Wireshark Network Security

A succinct guide to securely administer your network using Wireshark

Piyush Verma

BIRMINGHAM - MUMBAI

Wireshark Network Security

First published: July 2015

Production reference: 1240715

Published by Packt Publishing Ltd.
Livery Place
35 Livery Street
Birmingham B3 2PB, UK.

ISBN 978-1-78439-333-5

www.packtpub.com

Credits

Author
Piyush Verma

Reviewers
David Guillen Fandos

Mikael Kanstrup

Jaap Keuter

Tigran Mkrtchyan

Commissioning Editor
Amarabha Banerjee

Acquisition Editor
Larissa Pinto

Content Development Editor
Siddhesh Salvi

Technical Editor
Madhunikita Sunil Chindarkar

Copy Editor
Dipti Mankame

Project Coordinator
Nidhi Joshi

Proofreader
Safis Editing

Indexer
Priya Sane

Production Coordinator
Shantanu N. Zagade

Cover Work
Shantanu N. Zagade

About the Author

Piyush Verma currently serves as a senior security analyst at NII Consulting, India, and enjoys hacking his way into organizations (legally) and fixing the vulnerabilities encountered. He strongly values hands-on experience over certifications; however, here are a few certifications he has earned so far: OSCP, CEH, CHFI, CCNA Security, and CompTIA Security+. He is a highly sought-after professional speaker and has delivered security training to folks working in public, private, and "secret" sectors. He can be contacted at `https://in.linkedin.com/in/infosecpiyushverma`.

Acknowledgment

G.B. Stern quoted: "Silent gratitude isn't much use to anyone."

First and foremost, my deepest gratitude goes to my family, for being the perfect mix of love and chaos. My father, for his guidance and faith in my decisions; my mother, for her unconditional love and the awesome delicacies I much relish; and my sisters, for their love and support.

Thanks to these influential personalities in my journey so far: Mr. Dheeraj Katarya, my mentor, for all that you've taught me, which goes beyond the technical lessons; Mr. Sanjay Sharma, who is always a big motivator; Mr. Rahul Kokcha, for making the most difficult concepts easy to comprehend; Mr. Santosh Kumar, for his expert insights on Wireshark; Mr. K.K. Mookhey, for whom nothing is unachievable and he strives even bigger; Mr. Jaideep Patil, who is lavish in his praise and hearty in his approbation.

It has indeed been a pleasure to work with some of the great minds of the industry. Thanks to Mr. Wasim Halani, who has an answer for everything relevant and is rightly called the "Google" of our organization; Mr. Vikash Tiwary, for whom nothing matches his enthusiasm and the depth of knowledge he possesses. Special thanks to Saman, Parag, and Avinash for their feedback.

I'd also like to thank my friends, who made the most difficult times fun and fun times the most memorable.

Also, this book would have been difficult to achieve without the fantastic editorial team at Packt Publishing and the prodigious reviewers who helped bring out the best in me.

Ultimately, as the genius Albert Einstein quoted:

"I am thankful to all those who said *no*. It's because of them I did it myself."

About the Reviewers

David Guillen Fandos is a young Spanish engineer who enjoys being surrounded by computers and anything related to them. He pursued both his degrees, an MSc in computer science and an MSc in telecommunications, in Barcelona and has worked in the microelectronics industry since then.

He enjoys playing around in almost any field, including network security, software and hardware reverse engineering, and anything that could be considered security. Despite his age, David enjoys not-so-new technologies and finds himself working with compilers and assemblers. In addition to networking, he enjoys creating hacking tools to exploit various types of attacks.

David is now working at ARM after spending almost 2 years at Intel, where he does some hardware-related work in the field of microprocessors.

> I'd like to thank those people in my life who continuously challenge me to do new things, do things better than we do, or just change the way we look at life—especially those who believe in what they do and who never surrender no matter how hard it gets.

Mikael Kanstrup is a software engineer with a passion for adventure and the thrills in life. In his spare time, he likes kitesurfing, riding motocross, or just being outdoors with his family and two kids. Mikael has a BSc degree in computer science and years of experience in embedded software development and computer networking. For the past decade, he has been working as a professional software developer in the mobile phone industry.

Jaap Keuter has been working as a development engineer in the telecommunications industry for telephony to Carrier Ethernet equipment manufacturers for the past 2 decades. He has been a Wireshark user since 2002 and a core developer since 2005. He has worked on various internal and telephony-related features of Wireshark as well as custom-made protocol dissectors, fixing bugs and writing documentation.

Tigran Mkrtchyan studied physics at Yerevan State University, Armenia, and started his IT career as an X25 network administrator in 1995. Since 1998, he has worked at Deutsches Elektronen-Synchrotron (DESY)—an international scientific laboratory, located in Hamburg, Germany. In November 2000, he joined the dCache project, where he leads the development of the open source distributed storage system, which is used around the world to store and process hundreds of petabytes of data produced by the Large Hadron Collider at CERN. Since 2006, Tigran has been involved in IETF, where he takes an active part in NFSv4.1 protocol definition, implementation, and testing. He has contributed to many open source projects, such as the Linux kernel, GlassFish application server, Wireshark network packet analyzer, ownCloud, and others.

DESY is a national research center in Germany that operates particle accelerators used to investigate the structure of matter. DESY is a member of the Helmholtz Association and operates at sites in Hamburg and Zeuthen.

DESY is involved in the International Linear Collider (ILC) project. This project consists of a 30-km-long linear accelerator. An international consortium decided to build it with the technology developed at DESY. There has been no final decision on where to build the accelerator, but Japan is the most likely candidate.

www.PacktPub.com

Support files, eBooks, discount offers, and more

For support files and downloads related to your book, please visit www.PacktPub.com.

Did you know that Packt offers eBook versions of every book published, with PDF and ePub files available? You can upgrade to the eBook version at www.PacktPub.com and as a print book customer, you are entitled to a discount on the eBook copy. Get in touch with us at service@packtpub.com for more details.

At www.PacktPub.com, you can also read a collection of free technical articles, sign up for a range of free newsletters and receive exclusive discounts and offers on Packt books and eBooks.

https://www2.packtpub.com/books/subscription/packtlib

Do you need instant solutions to your IT questions? PacktLib is Packt's online digital book library. Here, you can search, access, and read Packt's entire library of books.

Why subscribe?

- Fully searchable across every book published by Packt
- Copy and paste, print, and bookmark content
- On demand and accessible via a web browser

Free access for Packt account holders

If you have an account with Packt at www.PacktPub.com, you can use this to access PacktLib today and view 9 entirely free books. Simply use your login credentials for immediate access.

Table of Contents

Preface

Wireshark is the tool of choice for network administration and troubleshooting, but its scalability goes beyond that. It is an excellent aid in performing an in-depth analysis of issues pertaining to the overall security of the network. Several tools and devices are available in the market to detect network-related attacks and take appropriate actions based on a predefined set of rules. However, at a very granular level, it all boils down to frames, or sometimes interchangeably called as packets, and the data they carry.

This book is written from the standpoint of using Wireshark to detect security-concerning flaws in commonly used network protocols and analyze the attacks from popular tools such as Nmap, Nessus, Ettercap, Metasploit, THC Hydra, and Sqlmap. In the later part of the book, we will dive into inspecting malware traffic from an exploit kit and IRC botnet and solve real-world Capture-The-Flag (CTF) challenges using Wireshark, basic Python code, and tools that complement Wireshark.

What this book covers

Chapter 1, Getting Started with Wireshark – What, Why, and How?, provides an introduction to sniffing and packet analysis and its purpose. Later, we will look at where Wireshark fits into the picture and how it can be used for packet analysis by performing our first packet capture.

Chapter 2, Tweaking Wireshark, discusses the robust features of Wireshark and how they can be useful in terms of network security. We will briefly discuss the different command-line utilities that ship with Wireshark.

Chapter 3, *Analyzing Threats to LAN Security*, dives into performing sniffing and capturing user credentials, analyzing network scanning attempts, and identifying password-cracking activities. In this chapter, we will also learn to use important display filters based on protocols and common attack-tool signatures and also explore regular expression-based filters. Then we will look at tools that complement Wireshark to perform further analysis and finally nail an interesting CTF challenge via the techniques learned in the chapter.

Chapter 4, *Probing E-mail Communications*, focuses on analyzing attacks on protocols used in e-mail communication and solving a couple of real-world e-mail communication challenges using Wireshark.

Chapter 5, *Inspecting Malware Traffic*, starts with creating a new profile under Wireshark for malware analysis and then picks up a capture file from an exploit kit in action and diagnoses it with the help of Wireshark. Later, we also give a brief on inspecting IRC-based botnets.

Chapter 6, *Network Performance Analysis*, begins by creating a troubleshooting profile under Wireshark and then discusses and analyzes TCP-based issues and takes up case studies of slow Internet, sluggish downloads, and delves further into picking up on Denial-of-Service attacks using Wireshark.

What you need for this book

To work with this book, you will need to download and install Wireshark on the operating system of your choice, and basic TCP/IP knowledge will be a plus.

Who this book is for

If you are a network administrator or a security analyst with an interest in using Wireshark for security analysis, this is the book for you. Basic familiarity with common network and application service terms and technologies is assumed; however, expertise in advanced networking topics or protocols is not required.

Conventions

In this book, you will find a number of text styles that distinguish between different kinds of information. Here are some examples of these styles and an explanation of their meaning.

Code words in text, database table names, folder names, filenames, file extensions, pathnames, dummy URLs, user input, and Twitter handles are shown as follows: "An indicator in that case will be the visibility of popular IRC commands as USER, NICK, JOIN, MODE, and USERHOST."

Any command-line input or output is written as follows:

```
frame contains "\x50\x4B\x03\x04"
```

New terms and **important words** are shown in bold. Words that you see on the screen, for example, in menus or dialog boxes, appear in the text like this: "To enable or disable the title, navigate to **Edit | Preferences | User Interface** and modify the option **Welcome screen and title bar shows version** to suit your requirement."

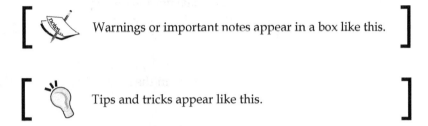

> Warnings or important notes appear in a box like this.

> Tips and tricks appear like this.

Reader feedback

Feedback from our readers is always welcome. Let us know what you think about this book—what you liked or disliked. Reader feedback is important for us as it helps us develop titles that you will really get the most out of.

To send us general feedback, simply e-mail feedback@packtpub.com, and mention the book's title in the subject of your message.

If there is a topic that you have expertise in and you are interested in either writing or contributing to a book, see our author guide at www.packtpub.com/authors.

Customer support

Now that you are the proud owner of a Packt book, we have a number of things to help you to get the most from your purchase.

Downloading the color images of this book

We also provide you with a PDF file that has color images of the screenshots/diagrams used in this book. The color images will help you better understand the changes in the output. You can download this file from https://www.packtpub.com/sites/default/files/downloads/3335OS_ColoredImages.pdf.

Errata

Although we have taken every care to ensure the accuracy of our content, mistakes do happen. If you find a mistake in one of our books—maybe a mistake in the text or the code—we would be grateful if you could report this to us. By doing so, you can save other readers from frustration and help us improve subsequent versions of this book. If you find any errata, please report them by visiting http://www.packtpub.com/submit-errata, selecting your book, clicking on the **Errata Submission Form** link, and entering the details of your errata. Once your errata are verified, your submission will be accepted and the errata will be uploaded to our website or added to any list of existing errata under the Errata section of that title.

To view the previously submitted errata, go to https://www.packtpub.com/books/content/support and enter the name of the book in the search field. The required information will appear under the **Errata** section.

Piracy

Piracy of copyrighted material on the Internet is an ongoing problem across all media. At Packt, we take the protection of our copyright and licenses very seriously. If you come across any illegal copies of our works in any form on the Internet, please provide us with the location address or website name immediately so that we can pursue a remedy.

Please contact us at copyright@packtpub.com with a link to the suspected pirated material.

We appreciate your help in protecting our authors and our ability to bring you valuable content.

Questions

If you have a problem with any aspect of this book, you can contact us at questions@packtpub.com, and we will do our best to address the problem.

1
Getting Started with Wireshark – What, Why, and How?

Sniffing and interpreting traffic on the network has been and always will be an integral part of a network analyst's job profile. It is not only restricted to the network analyst's profession, but it also plays a significant role in the fields of software development, network security, and digital forensics. Wireshark is the tool of choice at most workplaces and does not seem to slow down in terms of popularity and features, hence making it a "must-know" tool. This chapter gives a briefing on:

- Sniffing and its purpose
- Tools of the trade
- Getting up and running with Wireshark

Sniffing

Sniffing, by definition, is using our sense of smell to savor something, like a sniff of perfume. In this case, our nose acts as a sniffer. We can perform sniffing on the network using various tools categorized as packet sniffers to capture or collect the packets flowing in our networks. They are simply a way for us to see the network traffic and bandwidth information over the entire IT infrastructure. The technique of using a packet sniffer to sniff the data flowing over the wire or through thin air (wireless) is called packet sniffing.

The purpose of sniffing

Packet sniffing is performed in order to better understand what flows through our networks. Just as a poison flowing through the veins of the human body has the potential to kill an individual, similarly malicious traffic traversing our networks can have a severe and sometimes irreparable effect on the network devices, performance, and business continuity.

Sniffing helps a network analyst verify whether the implementation and functionality of the network and network security devices, such as the router, switch, firewall, IDS, or IPS, are as expected and also confirms that data is traversing through secure channels of communication.

Security analysts use sniffing to gather evidence in the case of a security breach with regard to the source of the attack, time and duration of the attack, protocols and port numbers involved, and data transmitted for the purpose of the attack. It can also help to prove the use of any insecure protocol(s) used to transmit sensitive information.

As Christopher Hitchens, a British-born American author, was once quoted saying:

> *"That which can be asserted without evidence, can be dismissed without evidence."*

Using a packet sniffer helps us get that piece of evidence.

Packet analysis

Now, to figure out whether the smell of the perfume is pleasant, ambrosial, or reeking is the analysis part. Hence, the art of interpreting and analyzing packets flowing through the network is known as packet analysis or network analysis. Mastering this art is a well-honed skill and can be achieved if a network administrator has a solid understanding of the TCP/IP protocol suite, is familiar with packet flows, and has an excellent grasp of any sniffer of choice.

Learning technology at the packet level helps to cement the most difficult concepts. For an easy example, let's say that a user wants to browse a website named example.com. As soon as the user enters the URL in the address bar and hits **GO**, the packets start to flow on the network with respect to that request. To understand this packet flow, we need to start sniffing to look at the packets in transit. The following screenshot shows the packets that traversed the network when the user opened example.com.

No.	Time	Source	Destination	Protocol	Length	Info
1	0.000000000	192.168.43.232	93.184.216.34	TCP	66	55736→80 [SYN] Seq=0 Win=8192 Len=0 MSS=1460 WS=4 SACK_PERM=1
2	0.428383000	93.184.216.34	192.168.43.232	TCP	66	80→55736 [SYN, ACK] Seq=0 Ack=1 Win=33320 Len=0 MSS=1360 WS=2 SACK_PERM=1
3	0.428490000	192.168.43.232	93.184.216.34	TCP	54	55736→80 [ACK] Seq=1 Ack=1 Win=66640 Len=0
4	0.428905000	192.168.43.232	93.184.216.34	HTTP	339	GET / HTTP/1.1
5	1.130966000	93.184.216.34	192.168.43.232	TCP	54	80→55736 [ACK] Seq=1 Ack=286 Win=66840 Len=0
6	1.152117000	93.184.216.34	192.168.43.232	HTTP	1001	HTTP/1.1 200 OK (text/html)
7	1.202033000	192.168.43.232	93.184.216.34	TCP	54	55736→80 [ACK] Seq=286 Ack=948 Win=65692 Len=0

We can analyze the packets after capturing them using a sniffer of choice, and in our case, we notice the columns that tell us about the source and destination IP addresses, the protocol being used, the length of the individual packets, and other relevant information. We will be digging into more detailed analysis as we progress though this book.

When we talk about enterprise networks, at any given point, there is humongous amount of traffic on the wire and analyzing such traffic is not a walk in the park. This traffic may be generated by numerous network devices communicating among each other, servers responding to user requests, or making their own requests over the Internet when required, and end users trying to accomplish their day-to-day tasks at work. There is no better way to understand this flow of information than to perform a packet-level analysis and, as the famous quote about network analysis goes, *packets never lie*. In addition, Gerald Combs, the man behind Wireshark, once tweeted the following:

> ""*The packets never lie*" *but as traffic volumes increase you end up with a trillion truths. The trick is finding the important ones.*"

Learning such tricks comes only with experience, as with anything else in the field of IT. As an example, if you want to improve your programming skills, you have to practice code writing day in and day out to be able to write structured and optimized pieces of code that can perform magic. The same goes for packet analysis.

Packet analysis can further help an administrator to:

- Monitor and provide a detailed statistics of activities on the network
- Distinguish between normal and unusual traffic
- Perform network diagnostics
- Identify and resolve network performance issues such as excessive bandwidth utilization
- Conduct deep packet inspection
- Investigate security breaches

The tools of the trade

There are numerous free and commercial packet sniffers, very often named network analyzers, in the market, and selecting the one that best meets your need is a matter of choice. There are several factors to determine this, such as the operating system in use, supported set of protocols, ease of use, customizability, and of course budget. The following are the popular ones:

- **Tcpdump**: Tcpdump is a free and popular command-line packet capture utility, which can come in very handy in the absence of a GUI-based tool. However, even after capturing traffic via tcpdump, one can analyze and interpret the traffic using any GUI-based free or commercial tool, as it is visually easy. Refer to TCPDUMP Overview at `http://www.tcpdump.org/manpages/tcpdump.1.html/`.

- **Nagios Network Analyzer and OmniPeek**: These are commercial-grade network analyzers that provide organizations with packet analysis capabilities with some unique features of their own. The pricing for these products can be seen on their individual websites.

- **Wireshark**: Wireshark, formerly known as Ethereal, is free and open source, and is the most popular packet analyzer out there. It works across multiple platforms and supports a huge set of protocol families with an easy-to-use GUI. Refer to `http://wiki.wireshark.org/ProtocolReference/`.

Apart from the dedicated sniffer tools we just introduced, packet sniffing capability and modules come integrated in many of the popular security-related tools, such as Snort, Metasploit, and Scapy, to name a few. Snort started off as a sniffer and later used its sniffing capabilities to develop into what we know today as the popular **network intrusion prevention system (NIPS)** and **network intrusion detection system (NIDS)** solution.

Another example is the presence of the `sniffer` module in Metasploit. After successfully compromising a machine using Metasploit, one can execute this module and start sniffing traffic on that compromised box for further enumeration. Sniffing options available with Metasploit are shown as follows:

```
Sniffer Commands
================

    Command             Description
    -------             -----------
    sniffer_dump        Retrieve captured packet data to PCAP file
    sniffer_interfaces  Enumerate all sniffable network interfaces
    sniffer_release     Free captured packets on a specific interface instead of downloading them
    sniffer_start       Start packet capture on a specific interface
    sniffer_stats       View statistics of an active capture
    sniffer_stop        Stop packet capture on a specific interface
```

Another excellent option is using `sniff()` in Scapy. Scapy is a packet manipulation tool written in Python and can be used to generate, craft, and decode packets and capture them. It is helpful in many security testing-related activities.

The focus of this book is "Wireshark". So, let's get started.

What is Wireshark?

Wireshark, as discussed earlier, is the most popular packet analyzer, and there is a reason behind its huge fan following. It hosts tons of features, supports a huge list of common and uncommon protocols with an easy-to-navigate GUI, and can be easily installed and used on popular operating systems, such as Windows, Linux, and Mac OS X for absolutely no cost at all.

Wireshark can be downloaded and installed from the official website (`http://www.wireshark.org`). The installation setup is comparatively simple, and within a few clicks, you will be up and running with Wireshark on a Windows machine.

 Installation guidelines for Windows, Unix, and Mac OS X can be found at `https://www.wireshark.org/docs/wsug_html_chunked/ChapterBuildInstall.html`.

As of writing this, the most recent version is Wireshark 1.12.6. Once downloaded and installed, you should be able to start Wireshark and will be presented with a screen similar to the one shown here:

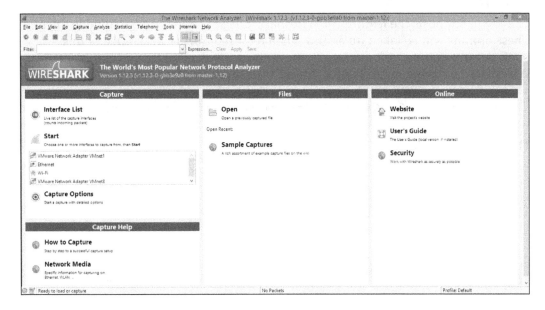

The Wireshark interface – Before starting the capture

Let's get started with various aspects of the Wireshark interface.

Title

This contains the default title of Wireshark along with the current version in use. To enable or disable the title, navigate to **Edit | Preferences | User Interface** and modify the option **Welcome screen and title bar shows version** to suit your requirement. To modify the title, navigate to **Edit | Preferences | User Interface | Layout** and enter a suitable title in the **Custom window title** field as shown in the following figure:

Custom window title (appended to existing titles):   Piyush Verma for PACKTPUB

The Wireshark Network Analyzer   [Piyush Verma for PACKTPUB]   [Wireshark 1.12.6 (v1.12.6-0-gee1fce6 from master-1.12)]

 Note: This will be appended to the current title as shown in the preceding screenshot.

Menu

The Menu bar hosts the features of Wireshark, all categorized under suitable titles. These options will be taken up as and when required during the course of this book. As an example, you can look at the authors involved in the development of Wireshark by navigating to **Help | About Wireshark** and selecting the **Authors** tab.

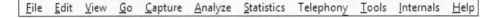

File   Edit   View   Go   Capture   Analyze   Statistics   Telephony   Tools   Internals   Help

This is how it will look:

Main toolbar

The main toolbar contains the icons for more frequently used items in Wireshark. You will note that some options are grayed out. This is because not all the options are available in the current context. Once we start the capture, we will see most of them highlighted and available for use.

Filter toolbar

Filtering the traffic can help analysts find a needle in a haystack. There are two types of filtering options available in Wireshark. One is called **capture filters**, and the second is called **display filters**.

Capture filters define which frames will be captured and sent to Wireshark's capture engine for processing and later displayed in Wireshark, while display filters define which frames are displayed after they are captured. We can redefine display filters without restarting the capture, which is not the case for capture filters; hence, we need to be cautious with their usage. The **Expression** option on the side helps us create the filter expressions in an easy way, as there is a huge list of filters, and we don't need to waste our time memorizing them.

Wireshark aids by providing visual indicators whether or not a filter used by us is correct (accepted by Wireshark), by changing the background color to *red* (wrong filter expression) and to *green* (correct filter expression) as shown in the following screenshot:

> ip.address == 192.168.1.1

Wrong filter

This is the correct filter will look something like this:

> ip.addr == 192.168.1.1

Correct filter

 You may notice that sometimes the filter shows a yellow background. This might be due to the fact that the filter expression which you entered is not working as expected. An example could be using ip.addr != 192.168.1.1 instead of the correct filter, that is, !(ip.addr == 192.168.1.1).

Once the filter expression is ready, you can either press **ENTER**, or click on **Apply** for that filter to be applied on the selected list of packets, and you can remove the current filter expression by clicking on **Clear**.

 Applying *display filters* on a large capture might take some time, and the progress is visible.

After spending some time creating filters, you will notice that you are combining a lot of them using multiple AND (&&) and OR (||) statements and would also want to use the same filter expression in another capture file. For this purpose, you can save your filters in Wireshark, using the **Save** button at the extreme right of filter toolbar.

Filter to see only HTTP GET requests made by 192.168.20.130

Capture frame

This frame helps in identifying the interface to start capturing packets from and the associated options with those interfaces.

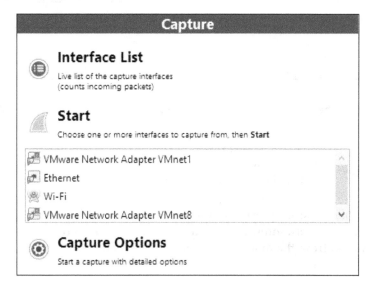

Here, at the capture frame, we have three ways to start capturing:

- **Interface List**: If you're not sure about the active interface to use for capture, selecting this option is a good choice as it gives you a complete list of the available interfaces, IP addresses in use, and the number of packets transmitted per interface. Using this information, we can easily figure out which interface to use to capture traffic.

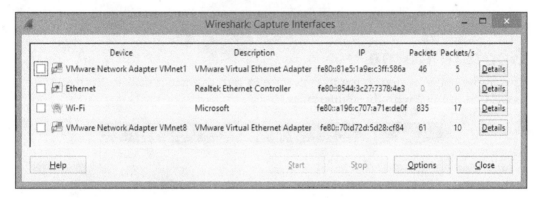

Simply ☑ the interface, and click on **Start** to begin the capture.

 You may choose to click on **Options** before starting the capture. However, this will open the same capture options discussed in **Capture Options**.

- **Start**: This is the simplest and quickest way to start the capture if you know the network interface(s) in question. All you need to do is select the interface(s) from the available list of interfaces and click on **Start**.

- **Capture Options**: This is an advanced way to start a capture, as it provides tweaking capabilities before a capture is even started.

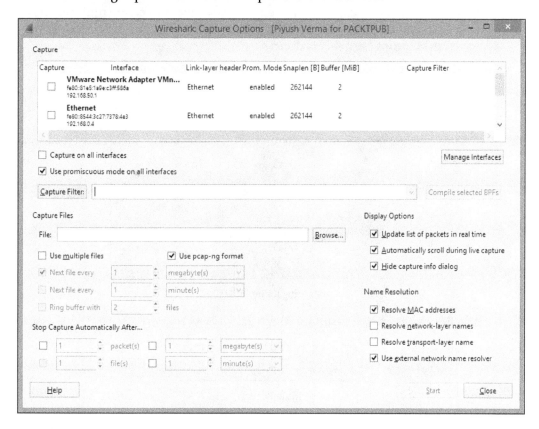

Here you can ☑ an individual interface to capture or ☑ **Capture on all interfaces**, to do exactly what it says.

By clicking on Capture Filter, you can select/create any filter before capturing begins. After this, you have some options that can be tweaked to perform unattended captures. For example, we want to create multiple files of 200 KB and stop the capture automatically after 2 minutes. The following screenshot shows how this is done:

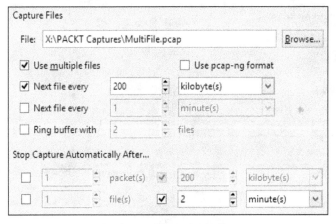

Configuring for multiple files

The following are the resultant files:

Multiple files

Wireshark saves the filename in `FileName_FileNumber_YEARMMDDHRMINSEC.pcap` format.

For details regarding the other options on this frame please go to `https://www.wireshark.org/docs/wsug_html_chunked/ChCapCaptureOptions.html`.

Capture Help

The following is how the **Capture Help** menu looks and later on we will see a description of the available options under this menu.

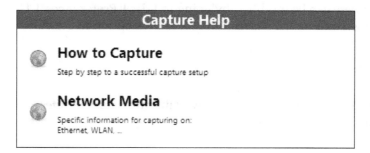

Here, we have two options that can help us with capturing using Wireshark in an efficient manner. Clicking on these options will redirect the user to:

- When the reader clicks on **How to Capture** they will be redirected to http://wiki.wireshark.org/CaptureSetup.

- When the reader clicks on **Network Media** they will be redirected to http://wiki.wireshark.org/CaptureSetup/NetworkMedia.

The Files menu

The following is how the **Files** menu looks and later on we will see a description of the available options under this menu.

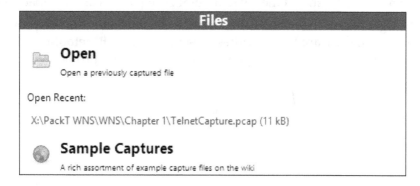

This menu provides options to:

1. Browse and open an already captured trace file.

2. Click and open any recently opened file. The number of recent files to be listed here can be modified by going to **Edit | Preferences | User Interface** and then editing the **Maximum recent files** option to the value of choice.

Maximum recent files:	5

3. Download sample capture files available at the official site (http://wiki.wireshark.org/SampleCaptures).

Online

As the name suggests, clicking on the options listed under this category redirects us to Wireshark's online resources.

The Status bar

The Status bar is used to display informational messages. It is divided into the following three sections:

- The left side of the Status bar shows context-related information, which includes the colorized bullet indicating the current expert-info level and an option to edit or add capture comments.

- The middle part shows the current number of packets and the load time.

- The right side of the Status bar shows the current configuration profile in use. By default, there are three profiles present [**Default**, **Bluetooth**, and **Classic**], and one can always create and use new configuration profiles as required.

File: "D:\PACKT Captures\MultiFile_00002_20150117125114.pcap" 129 kB 00:01:49   Packets: 483 · Displayed: 483 (100.0%) · Load time: 0:00.010   Profile: Default

Status bar

First packet capture

Let's get started with our first packet capture using Wireshark by following these steps:

1. Launch Wireshark

2. Select the correct interface to capture traffic. This can be done by navigating to the Menu bar and clicking on **Capture | Interfaces** (As a shortcut, we may choose *Ctrl + I*). Once we have the **Wireshark: Capture Interfaces** window open, perform the following steps:

    1. Select the Internet-facing interface (for example, Wi-Fi in my case). A good indication of the active interface is the **Packets** and **Packets/s** column on the right-hand side of the window as shown in the following screenshot:

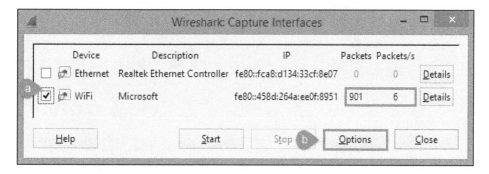

    2. After selecting the interface, click on the **Options** button, as highlighted in the screenshot, and the **Wireshark: Capture Options** window pops up as shown in the following screenshot:

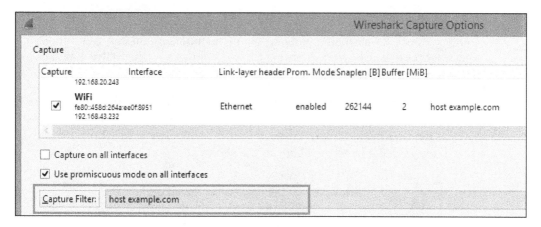

Enter host example.com in the **Capture Filter** field, as we only want to capture traffic to and from the domain example.com, and click on the **ENTER** key. We will discuss capture filters in detail in the next chapter.

3. The next step is to let Wireshark run in the background and open a browser of your choice (for example, Mozilla Firefox in my case) and browse example.com.

4. Once example.com loads, navigate to Wireshark, and stop the packet capture, by clicking on the **Stop** button ▪ in the main toolbar.

Once stopped, the capture appears as shown in the following screenshot:

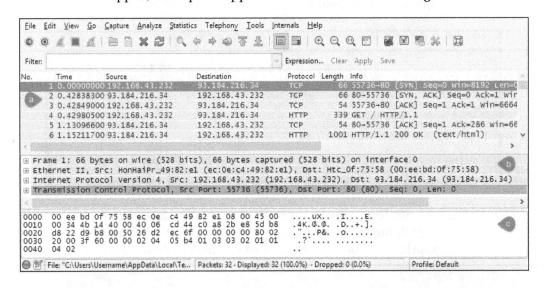

In the preceding screenshot, we can see Wireshark's menu bar, main toolbar and filter toolbar followed by three different panes and the Status bar. The three panes are as follows:

1. **Packet List pane**: This pane reflects the packets captured by Wireshark and some basic details about those packets. For example, the first packet in our capture is an SYN packet of the three-way handshake from the client to the server.

Please note that the packets displayed under this pane could be affected by the display filter, if any, used in the filter toolbar.

2. **Packet Details pane**: If we select any packet in the Packet List pane, its details are shown under this pane. For example, after selecting the first packet in our capture, we can look at the packet at a more granular level, that is, the changes it undergoes at different layers of networking (for example, source and destination ports under the Transmission Control Protocol (TCP), that is, the Transport layer of the TCP/IP model).

   This pane shows the protocols and protocol fields in a tree format and also displays any links when the current packet in question has a relationship to another packet in the same capture (for example, a request and response relationship for a single communication).

3. **Packet Bytes pane**: This pane displays the bytes of the selected packet in a hex dump format and is affected by what is selected in the previous pane, that is, the **Packet Details** pane.

5. The final step is to save the captured packets. We can do this by navigating to the menu bar, clicking on **File | Save** and saving it with an appropriate name in the directory of your choice.

Congratulations! With this, we have successfully captured and saved our first trace file.

Summary

In this chapter, we went over the foundations of sniffing and its practical importance in the real world, the different tools available at our disposal to perform sniffing, and understanding the Wireshark GUI to quickly get started with sniffing and perform our first packet capture. We shall begin the analysis part in the next chapter.

2
Tweaking Wireshark

It goes without saying that once you start sniffing on a busy network, you will be flooded with a bulk load of traffic, and in no time you may lose track of what you were looking for and seek assistance. Therefore, it becomes vital to understand the different features that come with the sniffer. This chapter will focus on such features while analyzing multiple trace files using Wireshark. At the end of this chapter, you will be comfortable with:

- Working with filters in Wireshark
- Creating multiple profiles
- Using advanced techniques
- Performing command-line fu with handy utilities that come prepackaged with Wireshark

Filtering our way through Wireshark

Filters are like conditionals that programmers/developers use while writing code. If we only wanted to see the ARP packets in the `TelnetCapture.pcap` file, we will apply a condition in the **Filter** toolbar for ARP and *if* the current file contains ARP packets, they will be displayed *else* no packets will be seen at all.

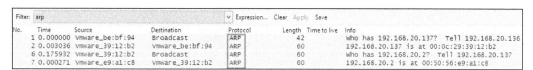

Only ARP traffic on display

The current stable version, 1.12.6, of Wireshark includes a total 13 default capture filters and 15 default display filters. To look at the list of available capture filters, we can go to the Menu bar, click on **Capture | Capture Filters...**, and to look at the available display filters, click on the **Filter** button on the **Filter** toolbar. We can use these as is, or we can use them as templates and customize them to add/create new ones to suit our needs.

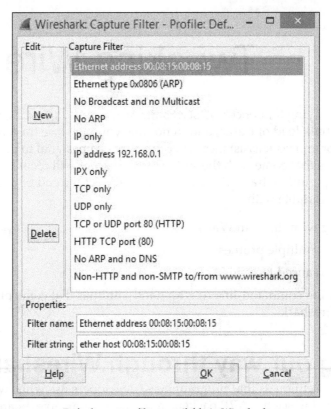

Default capture filters available in Wireshark

Wireshark provides the following two types of filtering options:

- Capture filters
- Display filters

The syntax for capture and display filters is different. Capture filters use **Berkeley Packet Filtering (BPF)** filter syntax also used by **tcpdump**, whereas display filters use Wireshark's specialized display filter format. To explore these filters in depth, please visit the following URLs:

Capture filters: `http://wiki.wireshark.org/CaptureFilters`

Display filters: `http://wiki.wireshark.org/DisplayFilters`

Capture filters

Capture filters are used before starting the capture on any interface and cannot be applied to an existing capture file.

When we know exactly what we're looking for, there is nothing better than capture filters. For example, when we need to troubleshoot **Dynamic Host Configuration Protocol (DHCP)**-related issues on a network and are not concerned with any other frames on the network, then we can apply the following capture filter: `port bootpc`, and all we will see is the DHCP traffic over the wire and nothing else.

Technically, all the traffic passes through the capture filter first and is then forwarded to the capture engine for further processing. In case a capture filter is applied, the frames that match the condition (capture filter) will be forwarded to Wireshark's **capture engine** and the rest will be completely discarded. This is the primary benefit of using capture filters as it offloads the computer from having to parse any useless frames. But this is a double-edged sword and we need to be careful when applying capture filters because we don't want to drop any frames that might be important from an analysis perspective.

Possessing an excellent set of capture filters in the arsenal can help us quickly pinpoint any anomaly on the network.

Another important point to be noted with respect to quick resolution of network issues is placing the analyzer at the right place, that is, **location**. As an example, if a lot of clients on the network complain about the network performance, then placing the analyzer closer to the server will be a good place to start, rather than analyzing at every client.

The following is a list of the capture filters:

Apart from the default set of the capture filters mentioned earlier, there are a number of capture filters that are handy to have in your arsenal. They are as follows:

Capture filter	Description
`ether host <Client's MAC> and ether host <Server's MAC>`	Client-and-server only traffic, based on their respective MAC addresses
`port bootpc`	DHCP only traffic
`vlan <vlan-id>`	For a specific VLAN
`ip6`	IPv6 only traffic
`ip proto 1`	ICMP only traffic
`port ftp`	FTP only traffic
`not port 3389`	Exclude RDP traffic
`udp dst port 162`	SNMP requests

The useful link to generate capture filters is `https://www.wireshark.org/tools/string-cf.html`.

 Whenever you're ambiguous about which capture filter to use, it is advisable to start off with a capture filter that is not too strict, or not use one at all and then narrow down the issue using display filters along the way. An example could be the use of the capture filter `udp dst port 162`, along with the display filter: `snmp.community`, to look at the community strings in the SNMP requests.

Display filters

Display filters are majorly used during analysis of already captured packets. However, they can also be used while capturing as they do not limit the packets being captured, they just restrict the visible number of packets.

Now, there will be times when we do not want to apply any filters before starting packet capture and need to capture everything that traverses our network.

For example, whenever a security incident is triggered on the network, it is important that we capture all the packets flowing on the wire and then analyze and reconstruct the event, using a packet/network analyzer tool such as Wireshark. During analysis, we might need to filter out traffic based on certain conditions, such as IRC-based communications or tracking down an FTP upload to a server in a different country. For the purpose of this, Wireshark provides **display filters** which makes life easier. Display filters allow us to take the maximum advantage of the Wireshark dissectors which take care of decoding and interpreting the fields of each packet.

There are tons of display filters available in Wireshark and memorizing them is not what we're supposed to do, luckily. In case we happen to know the field name, we can click on **Expressions** in the **Filter** toolbar and manually create one by selecting the **Field name** from the protocol subtree, the relation between the **Field name** and **Field value**, and then finally giving it a value.

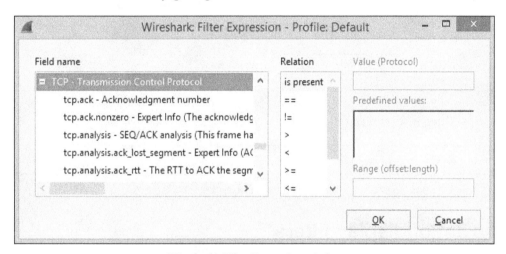

Wireshark's Filter Expression window

Another way is to simply select the specific packet, locate the field we're looking for in the **Packet Details** pane, and the respective **Field name** for the filter will be highlighted in the Status bar at the bottom.

As an example, we can see the following screenshot in which we are trying to find the **Field name** to use for filtering traffic based on TCP source port of 23.

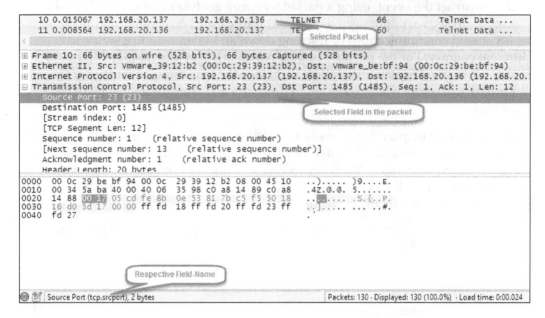

The final filter is shown as follows:

Display filter for source port -23 [TCP]

The list of display filters

The following table shows a handy set of display filters:

Display filter field names	Description
ip.addr	Traffic to or from an IP address
eth.addr	Traffic to or from an Ethernet address
tcp.port	Specify a TCP port
frame.time_delta	Time delta from the previous captured frame
http.request	HTTP requests only
arp.src.proto_ipv4	Sender IP in ARP packets
tcp.analysis.ack_rtt	Round-trip time
tcp.analysis.retransmission	Display all the retransmissions

Display filter field names	Description
`icmp.type`	Type of ICMP packet
`wlan.addr`	Hardware address [Ethernet or other MAC address]

For a more comprehensive list of display filters, you can refer to the following links:

- `https://www.wireshark.org/docs/dfref/`
- `http://packetlife.net/media/library/13/Wireshark_Display_Filters.pdf`

Wireshark profiles

As we get comfortable using Wireshark, we will be creating several filters along the way, and some of them will be pretty neat and useful in critical situations. Also, there will be situations when fixing a particular issue requires the use of multiple display and/or capture filters, various colorization schemes to highlight bad/ unexpected frames in the traffic assisting in visual distinction of such traffic, and customized preferences setting and layout changes. Therefore, creating our own profile for an attack scenario, a troubleshooting or any specific case is always a good option.

To look at the currently used profile in Wireshark, look at the bottom-right corner of the Status bar. So far, we have worked with the *Default* profile.

Creating a new profile

To create a new profile, press a combination of *Ctrl + Shift + A* on the keyboard and click on **New**, or go to **Edit | Configuration Profiles.** We can also right-click on the **Profile** area in the Status bar, and select **New**.

The following screenshot shows multiple profiles created for different scenarios, plus the **Switch To** option, which makes it easy to switch between multiple profiles swiftly:

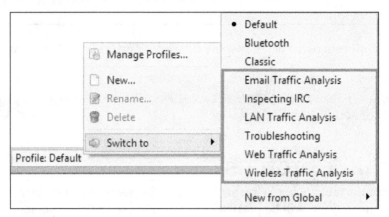

Newly created profiles are highlighted

Each profile configuration is located in different folders locally. To find the folder's location, simply go to **Help | About Wireshark** and select the **Folders** tab.

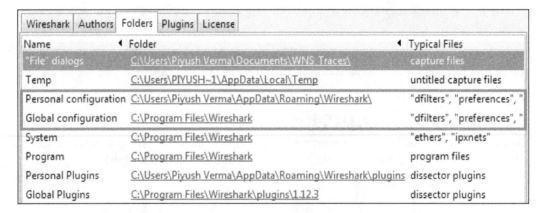

In the preceding screenshot, the highlighted portion contains the folder location for personal and global profiles.

In order to use your customized profile on another system, simply copy and paste the entire `profiles` folder to the other system's `profiles` folder.

Essential techniques in Wireshark

The techniques introduced under this section will provide you with the basic knowledge of what you will be dealing with, before diving deep into the packet analysis; these techniques are essential to understand from the packet analysis perspective. These mostly fall under the **Statistics** menu under the Menu bar as shown in the following figure:

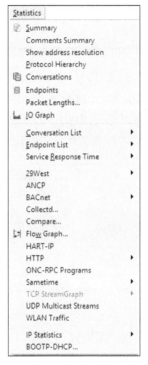

Numerous options under the Statistics category

The Summary window

To access the **Summary** window in Wireshark, go to **Statistics** in the Menu bar and select **Summary**. The **Summary** window includes the following:

- File details
- Time details
- Capture details
- Display details

Important details that can be deduced from here are:

- Capture time and duration
- Version details of operating system and Wireshark
- Capture interface
- Any capture/display filter used
- Average packets/sec, average packet size
- Average bytes/sec

The Protocol Hierarchy window

To view this, go to **Statistics** in the Menu bar and select **Protocol Hierarchy**. This section provides us with the distribution of protocols in the currently opened capture file, as follows:

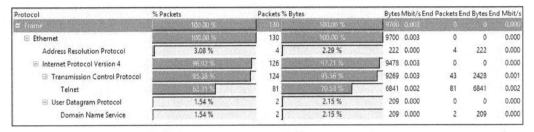

Protocol	% Packets		Packets	% Bytes		Bytes	Mbit/s	End Packets	End Bytes	End Mbit/s
Frame	100.00 %		130	100.00 %		9700	0.003	0	0	0.000
Ethernet	100.00 %		130	100.00 %		9700	0.003	0	0	0.000
Address Resolution Protocol	3.08 %		4	2.29 %		222	0.000	4	222	0.000
Internet Protocol Version 4	96.92 %		126	97.71 %		9478	0.003	0	0	0.000
Transmission Control Protocol	95.38 %		124	95.56 %		9269	0.003	43	2428	0.001
Telnet	62.31 %		81	70.53 %		6841	0.002	81	6841	0.002
User Datagram Protocol	1.54 %		2	2.15 %		209	0.000	0	0	0.000
Domain Name Service	1.54 %		2	2.15 %		209	0.000	2	209	0.000

Protocol Hierarchy statistics from TelnetCapture.pcapng

The Conversations window

A conversation is a communication between two entities or endpoints. Conversations can occur over different layers, as MAC layer, network layer, and transport layer. To view conversations, go to **Statistics | Conversations**.

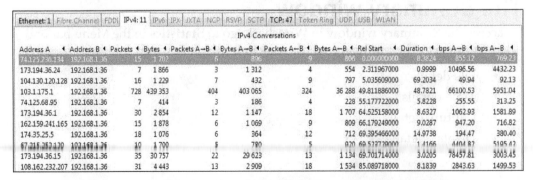

| Ethernet: 1 | Fibre Channel | FDDI | IPv4: 11 | IPv6 | IPX | JXTA | NCP | RSVP | SCTP | TCP: 47 | Token Ring | UDP | USB | WLAN |

IPv4 Conversations

Address A	Address B	Packets	Bytes	Packets A→B	Bytes A→B	Packets A→B	Bytes A→B	Rel Start	Duration	bps A→B	bps A→B
74.125.236.134	192.168.1.36	15	1 702	6	896	9	806	0.000000000	8.38.24	855.12	769.23
173.194.36.24	192.168.1.36	7	1 866	3	1 312	4	554	2.311967000	0.9999	10496.56	4432.23
104.130.120.128	192.168.1.36	16	1 229	7	432	9	797	5.035609000	69.2034	49.94	92.13
103.1.175.1	192.168.1.36	728	439 353	404	403 065	324	36 288	49.811886000	48.7821	66100.53	5951.04
74.125.68.95	192.168.1.36	7	414	3	186	4	228	55.177722000	5.8228	255.55	313.25
173.194.36.1	192.168.1.36	30	2 854	12	1 147	18	1 707	64.525158000	8.6327	1062.93	1581.89
162.159.241.165	192.168.1.36	15	1 878	6	1 069	9	809	66.179249000	9.0287	947.20	716.82
174.35.25.5	192.168.1.36	18	1 076	6	364	12	712	69.395466000	14.9738	194.47	380.40
67.215.253.170	192.168.1.36	10	1 700	5	780	5	920	69.533729000	1.4166	4404.82	5195.42
173.194.36.15	192.168.1.36	35	30 757	22	29 623	13	1 134	69.701714000	3.0205	78457.81	3003.45
108.162.232.207	192.168.1.36	31	4 443	13	2 909	18	1 534	85.089718000	8.1839	2843.63	1499.53

Conversation window for WebBrowsing.pcap

If we move over to the **TCP** tab, we will see the options that allow us to follow TCP streams and create graphs.

The Endpoints window

An endpoint is just one side of the conversation and it could be Ethernet, IPv4, and other options which are visible as tabs in the **Endpoints** window. Navigate to **Statistics | Endpoints** to look at the **Endpoints** window.

When we navigate to the **IPv4** tab of the **Endpoints** window, it shows us new columns such as **Country**, **City**, **Latitude**, and **Longitude**. In order to get these columns to reflect the values, we will need to configure GeoIP services first. Follow the steps mentioned later to configure GeoIP in Wireshark.

The following are the steps to configure GeoIP in Wireshark 1.12.6:

1. Download the GeoIP database. Since Wireshark does not prepackage its own set of GeoIP database(s), we will need to download a GeoIP database from `http://geolite.maxmind.com/download/geoip/database/`. This URL points to a freely available version of GeoIP database; however, you may also choose to buy it, if interested.

    Download the Binary/gzip files for GeoLite Country and GeoLite City from the earlier-mentioned URL and extract and save these in the directory of choice. Once extracted, they will look like the following:

2. Point Wireshark to the directory containing the GeoIP database. Launch Wireshark and navigate to **Edit | Preferences** and select **Name Resolution** under **User Interface** menu on the left-hand side of the window and click on **Edit** where it mentions **GeoIP database directories**, as highlighted in the following screenshot:

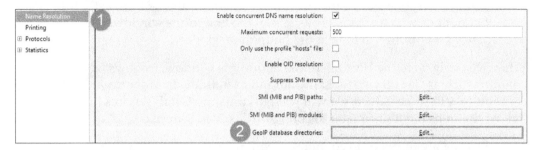

After clicking on **Edit**, we will be presented with the **GeoIP Database Paths** window and need to follow the steps highlighted in the following screenshot to mention the path to the directory holding the GeoIP databases, in my case D:\GeoIP.

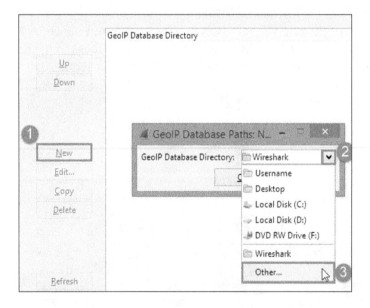

After selecting the path, click on **OK** and then again click on **OK** in the **GeoIP Database Paths** window to apply the path changes and finally the last **OK** in the **Wireshark Preferences** window.

3. Close Wireshark and relaunch it.

4. Open any trace file of choice, navigate to the **Endpoints** window, and click on **Map**, as highlighted in the following screenshot:

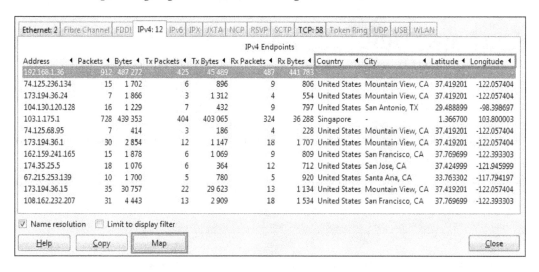

By clicking on **Map**, Wireshark uses the latitude and longitude values and creates a map on the fly. The following screenshot reflects a bird's eye view, however, if we zoom in we will be able to see the yellow dots spread further to their corresponding latitude and longitude values.

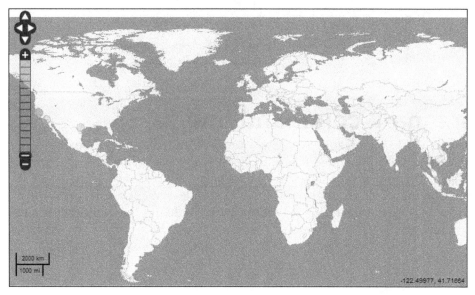

Yellow dots on the map show the locations pointed by the respective latitude and longitude shown in the Endpoints window

There are other interesting options under the **Statistics** category which we'll delve into every now and then during the course of this book.

The Expert Infos window

To open the **Expert Infos** window from the Menu bar navigate to **Analyze | Expert Info**, or simply click on the colored button on the left corner of the Status bar.

Wireshark uses **Expert Infos** to offer an expert advice in order to help us resolve problems and lead us to the root cause in some cases. This advice is categorized under **Errors**, **Warnings**, **Notes**, and **Chats** with **Errors** indicating the most severe problems and **Chats** showing the least.

The colored LEDs alongside these categories, as seen in the image earlier, are also present at the left corner of the Status bar indicating the level of severity for each packet.

Expert Info also has its own set of display filters as follows:

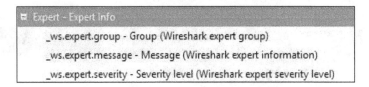

Wireshark command-line fu

In order to work conveniently with the command-line tools that come with Wireshark, it is recommended to add the path of the local Wireshark directory to the system environment variables. As we move ahead, I will assume that you've already configured the system environment variable as mentioned. Having said that, now let's look at the following more useful command-line utilities that ship with Wireshark:

* tshark
* capinfos
* editcap
* mergecap

Pass the -h argument with any of the command-line utilities to browse through the help options with each utility. For example, open the command prompt and run tshark -h.

tshark

The command-line version of Wireshark: **tshark** is used to capture and often display packets in typical situations when we don't have the privilege of using an interactive user interface, or when we are concerned about packet loss. Because in situations where a bulk load of traffic is flowing on the network, Wireshark's capture engine may not be able to capture at the speed with which the packets are thrown at the interface, and might crash as well. Hence, using tshark to capture such traffic is always a wise choice.

To look at all the options that are available with tshark, run the command tshark -h.

Starting the capture

If you run tshark without any parameters, it will start capturing on the first non-loopback interface it encounters. To look at the available interfaces, we can run the following command:

```
C:\>tshark -D
```

```
C:\>tshark -D
1. \Device\NPF_{A0A69947-9A6A-4B5F-87EE-900B6F7D307A} (VMware Network Adapter VM
net1)
2. \Device\NPF_{A0CC0E6D-5F3A-49EB-9AC7-9A8DBDFA5FDA} (Ethernet)
3. \Device\NPF_{A2BD2764-92CC-4DAB-A414-655ED62450C1} (Wi-Fi)
4. \Device\NPF_{8D64E150-0BD8-46F0-8454-5B9577DE25C9} (Local Area Connection)
```

Listing the interfaces with tshark

Simply select the interface you want to use and start capturing the traffic on that interface (in this case, 2) by running the following command:

```
C:\>tshark -i 2
```

 Stopping the capture

To stop manually, press the combination of *Ctrl* + *C*.

To stop automatically, use -a option with a condition. The capture stops when the applied condition is met. For example, the following capture stops after 10 seconds:

```
C:\>tshark -i 2 -a duration:10
```

Saving the capture to a file

Now, there will be times when you need to save the packets captured in a file. In that case you can use the -w option:

```
C:\>tshark -i 2 -w FirstCapture.pcap
```

Using filters

You can use both display and capture filters while capturing traffic using tshark.

To use capture filters with tshark, use the -f option as given in the following:

```
C:\>tshark -i 2 -f "port bootpc" -w DHCP_Only.pcap
```

To use display filters with tshark, use the -R option as given in the following:

```
C:\>tshark -2 -R "http.request.method==GET" -r HTTP_Traffic.pcap -w HTTP_
Get.pcap
```

Using the above command we're reading HTTP_Traffic.pcap, applying a display filter of http.request.method==GET and then writing the filtered packets to HTTP_Get.pcap.

Statistics

tshark also gives us an option to view the statistics by using the -z parameter.

To view the **Protocol Hierarchy**, use the following option:

```
C:\>tshark -r HTTP_Traffic.pcap -qz io,phs
```

```
C:\Users\Piyush Verma>tshark -r HTTP_traffic.pcap -qz io,phs

==========================================================================
Protocol Hierarchy Statistics
Filter:

eth                                      frames:721 bytes:598880
  ip                                     frames:721 bytes:598880
    tcp                                  frames:721 bytes:598880
      http                               frames:86 bytes:56115
        data-text-lines                  frames:10 bytes:8063
          tcp.segments                   frames:6 bytes:3501
        media                            frames:10 bytes:8649
          tcp.segments                   frames:9 bytes:7535
        png                              frames:22 bytes:16904
          tcp.segments                   frames:21 bytes:16002
        image-gif                        frames:1 bytes:1390
        urlencoded-form                  frames:1 bytes:733
==========================================================================
```

capinfos

capinfos is used to print the capture file's information as follows:

```
C:\Users\Piyush Verma>capinfos -tcsyizH HTTP_Traffic.pcap
File name:             HTTP_Traffic.pcap
File type:             Wireshark/tcpdump/... - pcap  ← -t
Number of packets:     721  ← -c
File size:             610 kB  ← -s                               -H
Data byte rate:        6465 bytes/s  ← -y
Data bit rate:         51 kbps  ← -i                               ↓
Average packet size:   830.62 bytes  ← -z
SHA1:                  40d6829e50a407f0f993ad2a822a3259e8d31833
RIPEMD160:             c912b71a9cbae82f9c5d3252d9e0fb7a9e28f1fc
MD5:                   2a7d11176fc4802e9f84f8d3b1f84d48
```

Most commonly used options used with capinfos

The `-H` parameter is used to create hash of the capture file using the commonly used hashing algorithms [`SHA1`, `RIPEMD160`, and `MD5`].

We can either use these arguments individually or combine them as shown in the preceding.

> You can run the capinfos command without passing any argument, to look at the abstract summary of the capture file, as follows:
>
> **capinfos HTTP_Traffic.pcap**

editcap

This utility comes in handy when modifying capture files, such as splitting up a large file into multiple file sets, removing duplicate packets from a file, or converting a capture file from one format into another.

```
C:\Users\Piyush Verma>editcap -v -c 400 HTTP_Traffic.pcap HTTP.pcap
```

HTTP_00000_20150210215026	2/12/2015 11:05 AM	Wireshark capture file	328 KB
HTTP_00001_20150210215047	2/12/2015 11:05 AM	Wireshark capture file	282 KB
HTTP_Traffic	2/10/2015 9:53 PM	Wireshark capture file	597 KB

Splitting a file into multiple file sets using editcap

The following example shows how to remove duplicate packets from a trace file [`Duplicates.pcap`]. This is generally done to save from the trouble of going over the same packets repeatedly and hence shorten the analysis time.

```
C:\>editcap -d Duplicates.pcap NoDuplicates.pcap
```

mergecap

This utility is majorly used to combine multiple capture files into a single output file. As can be seen in the following screenshot, two PCAP files were given as input to the `mergecap` utility which generated an amalgamated version named 'HTTP_Merged.pcap'.

```
C:\Users\Piyush Verma>mergecap HTTP_00000_201502210215026.pcap HTTP_00001_2015021
0215047.pcap -w HTTP_Merged.pcap
```

HTTP_00000_201502102155026	2/12/2015 11:05 AM	Wireshark capture file	328 KB
HTTP_00001_201502102155047	2/12/2015 11:05 AM	Wireshark capture file	282 KB
HTTP_Merged	2/12/2015 10:24 PM	Wireshark capture file	609 KB

Combining multiple HTTP capture files into HTTP_Merged.pcap

Summary

In this chapter, we looked at the power of using capture filters in a busy network and how to find our way through a big trace file using display filters or simply splitting it into multiple files for easy navigation. We also created new profiles in Wireshark to help us ease our day-to-day activities and learned how to use the awesome command-line utilities that are shipped with Wireshark. We will be using these as well as the advanced techniques as we move ahead further in this book. In the next chapter, we will analyze threats to LAN security.

3
Analyzing Threats to LAN Security

"Knowing yourself is the beginning of all wisdom"

Aristotle

Having a crystal clear picture of what flows through our network is significant to understanding any suspicious traffic traversing the wire. In simple words, we should be able to distinguish between good and bad traffic. Baselining good traffic is an important step in this direction and can significantly reduce the effort required for threat analysis. In this chapter, we will go over threats to LAN security and how we can use Wireshark to analyze them. We will also solve a real-world **Capture The Flag (CTF)** challenge at the end.

LAN is our own kingdom, and we, the soldiers of this kingdom, are obligated to maintain a nonhostile environment. As with any kingdom, threats are always present and are not easy to eradicate. There are many vectors from where a threat can arise, for example, the mischievous people of the kingdom, from enemies in the outside world, and so on.

Now, fast-forwarding time and in the real world where the kingdom is the organization we are employed by and where threats can arise from eventually anywhere, such as natural disasters, disgruntled employees, anyone on the outside or even a rat biting off your network cable. Yes, a rat biting off the cable is a threat but definitely not one that you can analyze via Wireshark.

Security threats have been relentlessly inventive with different attack vectors and are constantly evolving. The countermeasures are numerous with a pool of companies providing security solutions in the form of software- and hardware-based solutions to prevent and detect such attacks. Detecting these attacks is as important as preventing them, and when we speak of an enterprise, the tools they instill their faith in are preconfigured with some sort of sniffing functionality integrated in them. Examples of such tools that integrate sniffing features have been discussed earlier. Automation is good, and I am a big preacher of that myself, but complete reliance on tools is also not a smart approach and as far as detecting network attacks is concerned, it is a good bet to have someone analyze the traffic as it flows. Also, Wireshark, with its extensive set of features, as discussed in the previous chapters, can help us detect the majority of the attacks occurring over the network.

Let's begin by analyzing clear-text traffic.

Analyzing clear-text traffic

First up we will look at the clear-text traffic that traverses our network. The biggest security issue with such traffic is the human-readable and understandable format it is in, even sensitive information as user credentials. Clear-text traffic can be easily understood by human beings without any additional processing, as we will see under this section. Many common protocols in our networks communicate in such a manner. The following is the list of commonly used protocols:

- FTP
- Telnet
- HTTP
- TFTP
- SMTP
- POP3

Viewing credentials in Wireshark

Now, we will look at how to view credentials for these clear-text protocols individually.

FTP

File Transfer Protocol (FTP), is used to transfer files over TCP and by default runs over port 21, unless customized to use a different port. It is one of the most common protocols used for file transfer. The following is a capture of an FTP communication showing user credentials in the packet lists pane of Wireshark:

```
5 0.001510000  192.168.20.129   192.168.20.200   TCP   49944→21 [ACK] Seq=1 Ack=28 Win=29696 L
6 3.285827000  192.168.20.129   192.168.20.200   FTP   Request: USER anonymous
7 3.286395000  192.168.20.200   192.168.20.129   FTP   Response: 331 Anonymous access allowed,
8 3.286570000  192.168.20.129   192.168.20.200   TCP   49944→21 [ACK] Seq=17 Ack=100 Win=29696
9 5.610442000  192.168.20.129   192.168.20.200   FTP   Request: PASS anonymous
10 5.611472000 192.168.20.200   192.168.20.129   FTP   Response: 230 Anonymous user logged in.
```

FTP credentials in clear-text

Telnet

Telnet is a protocol generally used to interact with a remote computer. It has been the most common way to configure network devices or control web servers remotely. Data again travels over clear-text when Telnet is used, but luckily we're shifting to the use of more secure protocols such as SSH to remotely manage and communicate with devices.

Telnet runs over TCP port 23 by default.

Steps to view credentials for the Telnet traffic are as follows:

1. Go to **Statistics | Conversations** and move over to the **TCP** tab.

2. Select the appropriate Telnet conversation (indication is port 23) and click on **Follow Stream** at the bottom.

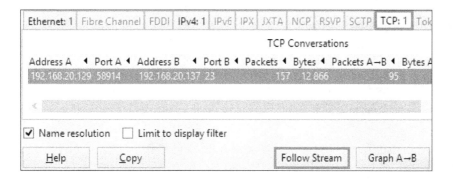

After following the TCP stream, we can clearly see the Telnet traffic along with the credentials as follows:

```
metasploitable login: mmssffaaddmmiinn
.
Password: msfadmin
```

> By default, *red* color in the TCP stream indicates the data sent from the client and *blue* indicates the data sent by the server. Hence, we're presented with an odd looking username, which is a combination of a byte sent and received. If we separate and look at those bytes individually, we can easily figure out the username.

HTTP

Hyper Text Transfer Protocol (HTTP) is a popular application layer protocol commonly used to browse websites and transfer hypertext documents between a web server and a client (generally, a web browser).

By default, HTTP uses TCP port 80 and since many organizations prefer to use custom ports for their web services Wireshark has included a list of some common ports that it dissects as HTTP traffic. These can be found and further edited under **Edit | Preferences | Protocols | HTTP**.

TCP Ports:	80,3128,3132,5985,8080,8088,11371,1900,2869,2710
SSL/TLS Ports:	443

> Recently, HTTP upgraded from 1999's HTTP/1.1 to HTTP/2, and as of this writing, there is no official start date for the use of HTTP/2, but many might unknowingly still be using it. The latest servers (IIS under Windows 10) and browsers (Firefox Beta 36) are said to have already started support for HTTP/2.

HTTP traffic also travels in plain text, and it doesn't matter what type of request (GET or POST) is being used: none of them are secure, as the protocol itself does not provide any sort of encryption. Hence, we use HTTPS (HTTP over SSL/TLS) to send over sensitive information.

HTTPS is a secure alternative to HTTP, but it will be naïve to say that using HTTPS secures everything, as we have recently seen vulnerabilities being discovered against SSL and TLS, namely HeartBleed, BEAST, CRIME, POODLE, and FREAK making SSL v3.0 an obsolete and insecure protocol.

Later in the chapter, we will look at a notorious attack, which uses a different vector from the attacks mentioned earlier. Under this attack, we will strip off SSL from HTTPS, hence turning it into HTTP [clear-text form] and making it easy for us to read and understand the communication.

TFTP

We will almost always need a reliable protocol to transfer files; hence, we will use FTP or, now that we're aware of rather secure alternatives, we may want to choose from them. But we will rarely use TFTP as it works over UDP and since UDP is an unreliable protocol, it is not recommended for file transfers.

You will notice very rare TFTP traffic over the wire. For example, one of the ways to transfer an IOS image to a Cisco device is by using TFTP protocol and you don't do that very often. Do you?

Bottomline: TFTP is an unusual protocol to be seen on the network, and we need to make sure that we analyze such traffic carefully whenever we encounter such traffic crossing the wire.

Reassembling data stream

When traffic is traversing in clear-text, it becomes an easy task to reassemble data in order to see to which files are being transferred or downloaded over the network. An example case study, where honing these skills can be helpful, is shared later.

Case study

In a recent forensic investigation I was involved in, we were asked to take care of a fraud. After going over the requested data provided by the organization, I decided to analyze the capture files.

During analysis of these capture files, something caught my attention. I noted file transfers occurring at a specific time on every alternate day. These transfers happened over FTP, from a client machine inside the company to an external IP address, which was unknown to the organization.

My next step was to pull out the transferred data from the TCP streams (reassemble FTP data stream), and for that, I followed the steps similar to the following ones:

1. Check the TCP conversations. Sort the conversations based on the maximum **Bytes** transferred and select and follow the suspicious looking stream (generally on the basis of huge number of bytes transferred) by clicking on **Follow Stream** as follows:

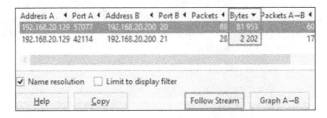

2. After looking at the stream, you need to select the correct direction/flow of data by looking at the bytes transferred as follows:

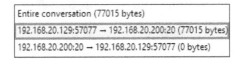

3. Once selected, the next step is to identify the file being transferred by analyzing the stream for a file signature, and in this case it is JFIF, which is an indicator of a JPG file.

4. The final step is to save the stream by clicking on **Save As** and saving it in the identified format. In this case, I saved it as a JPG file.

The case was solved by first reassembling data and extracting an image file and then analyzing it, only to narrow down that an XLS file was hidden behind that image using a technique known as **Steganography**.

Steganography is the science of hiding/concealing data within other seemingly harmless messages.

Advanced Forensics Toolkits and open source tools are available to analyze and extract information and files from the capture files. However, this was an example of how Wireshark can be handy in such a case.

Data streams can be reassembled in similar fashion for other clear-text protocols as well.

> SMTP and POP3 are covered in brief in the next chapter, that is, *Chapter 4, Probing E-mail Conversations*.

Examining sniffing attacks

Sniffing activities are performed by malicious users / attackers in a **Man-in-the-Middle (MitM)** scenario where they want to grasp data flowing on the network. There are two types of sniffing attacks:

- Passive sniffing
- Active sniffing

Passive sniffing refers to sniffing on a hubbed network, where all devices on the network are connected to a hub and since all the packets are sent to all the connected devices on a hub, the attacker simply needs to plug into that hub and listen to the conversations occurring over that hub. It is easy to sniff on a network that uses a hub, but it is very rare to find a hubbed network.

Active sniffing refers to sniffing on a switched network, where the devices are connected to a switch, and a switch, unlike a hub, does not broadcast all the packets to all the devices on the network. Hence, it is not as easy to perform sniffing on a network that uses a switch. Yet, it is not impossible to perform it on a switched network either.

In the current environments where switches are used, we cannot just plug in a laptop and start the sniffer. In fact, even plugging in the laptop and getting access to the network is not easy with many **Network Access Control (NAC)**-based solutions around, leave alone starting a sniffer on that.

To sniff on a switch-based environment, an attacker needs to perform additional attacks. In this case, we assume that the attacker is an insider or someone who has enough privileges on the LAN to perform these attacks. The attacks are as follows:

- MAC flooding
- ARP poisoning

MAC flooding

MAC flooding, also known as CAM table exhaustion attack, is an attack where an attacker floods the switch with a large quantity of random MAC addresses so as to fill the CAM table of the switch. This attack takes advantage of the limited memory a switch has to maintain the mapping of MAC addresses to its physical ports, and when this attack succeeds, the switch turns into a hub and starts sending the packets to all ports making it easy for the attacker to sniff the traffic on the wire.

Tools used for this attack are Macof and Yersinia.

Detect MAC flooding attacks with Wireshark:

Wireshark's Expert Info: In case of a MAC flooding attack, first of all Wireshark marks all packets as malformed packets, and this is visible under the **Expert Info** window also as follows:

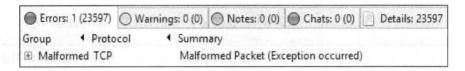

Now, let's look at some other indications of a MAC flood in the following screenshot:

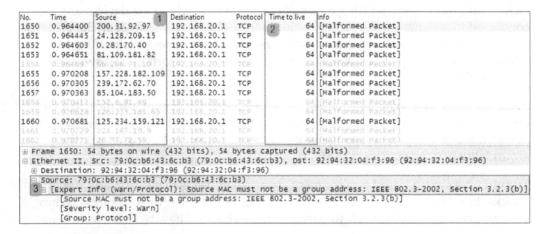

- Here random source IP addresses (1) with the same TTL value (2), well that raises an eyebrow, and that too to the same destination in this case.

- There are also a lot of frames with source MAC addresses belonging to IEEE 802.3-2002 group (display filter: eth.bro_not_group).

ARP poisoning

Address Resolution Protocol (ARP), is used to resolve a device's MAC address from a known IP address, and a point to note is that ARP requests are broadcasts while ARP replies are unicasts.

ARP poisoning is a very common MitM attack method. During this attack, the MAC address of the attacker is associated with the IP address of the target host or to all the hosts on the network, depending on the type of chosen attack. The following snapshot shows the ARP cache table of one of the hosts when the attack is in progress:

```
Interface: 192.168.20.132 --- 0xb
  Internet Address      Physical Address      Type
  192.168.20.1          00-0c-29-9b-1a-7a      dynamic
  192.168.20.2          00-0c-29-9b-1a-7a      dynamic
  192.168.20.128        00-0c-29-9b-1a-7a      dynamic
  192.168.20.129        00-0c-29-9b-1a-7a      dynamic
  192.168.20.135        00-0c-29-9b-1a-7a      dynamic
```

The tools required are Ettercap, Arpspoof and Cain and Abel.

The following are the steps to detect ARP poisoning attacks with Wireshark:

- Look for **Duplicate IP address configured** in the **Expert Info** window's **Warnings** tab as shown in the following screenshot:

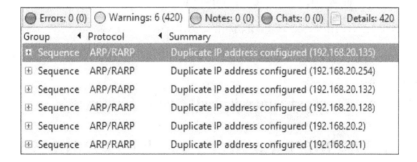

Otherwise, filter traffic using `arp.duplicate-address-detected`.

- We can also filter the packets that have the gateway's IP address but not the gateway's MAC address, because generally the attacker attempts to fake the gateway's MAC address. Wireshark's display filter for this will be:

`arp.src.proto_ipv4 == <Gateway's IP> && !(eth.src == <Gateway's MAC address>)`

Analyzing network reconnaissance techniques

The dictionary definition of **reconnaissance** is *military observation of a region to locate an enemy or ascertain strategic features*. A good analogy for reconnaissance will be a thief studying the neighborhood to observe which houses are empty and which ones are occupied, the number of family members who live at the occupied houses, their entry points, the time during which these occupied houses are empty, and so on before he/she even thinks about stealing anything from that neighborhood.

Network reconnaissance relates to the act of gathering information about the target's network infrastructure, the devices that reside on the network, the platform used by such devices and the ports opened on them, to ultimately come up with a brief network diagram of devices and then plan the attack accordingly.

Next, we will detect such activities using Wireshark.

Examining network scanning activities

The tools required to perform network scanning activities are readily available and can be downloaded easily from the Internet. One such popular tool is **Network Mapper (Nmap)**. It is written by Gordon "Fyodor" Lyon and is a popular tool of choice to perform network-based reconnaissance.

Network scanning activities can be as follows:

- Scanning for live-machines
- Port scans
- Detecting presence of a firewall or additional IP protocols

Detect the scanning activity for live machines

An attacker would want to map out the live machines on the network rather than performing any activity with an assumption that all the machines are live. Following are the two popular techniques that can be used and the ways to detect them using Wireshark.

Ping sweep

This technique makes use of a simple technique to ping an IP address in order to identify whether it is alive or not. Almost all modern networks block the ICMP protocol; hence, this technique is not very successful. However, in case your network supports ICMP-based traffic, you can detect this attack by looking for large number of ping requests going to a range of IP addresses on your network. A helpful filter in this case will be:

```
icmp.type == 8 || icmp.type == 0
ICMP Type 8 = ECHO Request
ICMP Type 0 = ECHO Reply
```

ARP sweep

ARP responses cannot be disabled on the network; hence, this technique works very well while trying to identify live machines on a local network. Using this technique, an attacker can discover hosts that may be hidden from other discovery methods, such as ping sweeps, by a firewall.

To perform this, an attacker sends an ARP broadcast (destination MAC address—FF:FF:FF:FF:FF:FF) for all the possible IP addresses on a given subnet, and the machines responding to these requests are noted as alive or active.

To detect ARP sweep attempts, we need to look for a massive amount of ARP broadcasts from a client machine on the network. Another thing to note will be the duration in which these broadcasts are sent. These are highlighted in the following screenshot:

No.	Time	Source	Destination	Protocol	Length	Info
200	*REF*	Vmware_e7:a7:32	Broadcast	ARP	42	who has 192.168.20.239? Tell 192.168.20.128
201	0.001763	Vmware_e7:a7:32	Broadcast	ARP	42	who has 192.168.20.211? Tell 192.168.20.128
202	0.003438	Vmware_e7:a7:32	Broadcast	ARP	42	who has 192.168.20.205? Tell 192.168.20.128
203	0.004951	Vmware_e7:a7:32	Broadcast	ARP	42	who has 192.168.20.197? Tell 192.168.20.128
204	0.007426	Vmware_e7:a7:32	Broadcast	ARP	42	who has 192.168.20.184? Tell 192.168.20.128
205	0.009151	Vmware_e7:a7:32	Broadcast	ARP	42	who has 192.168.20.243? Tell 192.168.20.128
206	0.010861	Vmware_e7:a7:32	Broadcast	ARP	42	who has 192.168.20.179? Tell 192.168.20.128
207	0.012412	Vmware_e7:a7:32	Broadcast	ARP	42	who has 192.168.20.163? Tell 192.168.20.128
208	0.014607	Vmware_e7:a7:32	Broadcast	ARP	42	who has 192.168.20.136? Tell 192.168.20.128
209	0.017888	Vmware_e7:a7:32	Broadcast	ARP	42	who has 192.168.20.123? Tell 192.168.20.128

An ARP sweep in action

 A point to note is the source of these ARP requests to avoid false positives because such requests can also be made by legitimate services such as SNMP.

Identify port scanning attempts

Now, we will look at different port scanning techniques used by attackers and how to detect them using Wireshark.

A TCP Connect scan

In a TCP Connect scan, a client/attacker sends a SYN packet to the server/victim on a range of port numbers. For the ports that respond with SYN/ACK, the client completes the three-way handshake by sending an ACK and then terminates the connection by sending an RST to the server/victim, while the ports that are closed reply with RST/ACK packets to the SYN sent by the client/attacker.

Hence, in order to identify this type of scan, we will need to look for a significantly large number of RST (**Expert Info**) or SYN/ACK packets. In general, when a connection is established, some form of data is transferred; however, in scanning attempts no data is sent across, indicating that someone is performing a scan (navigate to **Conversations | TCP**).

Another indication is the short period of time under which these packets are sent; navigate to **Statistics | Flow Graph**.

Wireshark's Flow Graph

While observing the TCP flow in the **Flow Graph**, we noted a sequence of SYN, SYN/ACK, and ACKs along with SYN and RST/ACKs. Another indication is the fraction of seconds (displayed on the left-hand side) under which these packets are sent.

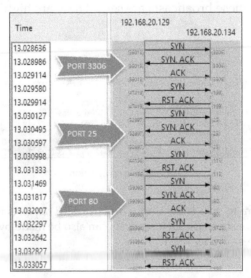

A complete three-way handshake with open ports and how quickly
the packets were sent under the "Time" column

Wireshark's Expert Info

Even the **Expert Info** window indicates a significant number of connection resets.

Errors: 0 (0)	Warnings: 1 (946)	Notes: 0 (0)	Chats: 1012 (1012)	Details: 1958	Packet Comments: 0
Group ◀	Protocol ◀	Summary		◀ Count	◀
⊞ Sequence	TCP	Connection reset (RST)			946

The Warning tab under Expert Info

Wireshark's Conversations

We can look at the TCP conversations, to observe which type of scan is underway and the number of bytes associated with each conversation.

Address A ◀	Port A ◀	Address B ◀	Port B ◀	Packets ▼	Bytes ◀
192.168.20.129	51610	192.168.20.134	53	4	280
192.168.20.129	38185	192.168.20.134	21	4	280
192.168.20.129	37020	192.168.20.134	3306	4	280
192.168.20.129	56592	192.168.20.134	23	4	280
192.168.20.129	60096	192.168.20.134	80	4	280
192.168.20.129	53907	*Open Ports*	25	4	280
192.168.20.129	43531	192.168.20.134	22	4	280
192.168.20.129	35940	192.168.20.134	139	4	280
192.168.20.129	51495	192.168.20.134	445	4	280
192.168.20.129	36845	192.168.20.134	8180	4	280
192.168.20.129	42382	192.168.20.134	8009	4	280
192.168.20.129	50915	192.168.20.134	5432	4	280
192.168.20.129	43550	192.168.20.134	143	2	134
192.168.20.129	5499	*Closed Ports*	1723	2	134
192.168.20.129	48423	192.168.20.134	199	2	134
192.168.20.129	39179	192.168.20.134	256	2	134

The number of packets and Bytes transferred for each conversation

The number 4 in the **Packets** column indicates a SYN, SYN/ACK, ACK, and RST packets, and the number 2 indicates the SYN sent by Nmap and RST/ACK received for a closed port.

Stealth scan

A stealth scan is different than the TCP Connect scan explained earlier and is never detected by the application layer, as the complete TCP three-way handshake is never established during this scan and hence a.k.a. half-open scan.

During this scan, a client/attacker sends a SYN packet to the server/victim on a range of port numbers. If Nmap receives a SYN/ACK to the SYN request, it means that the port is open; then, Nmap sends an RST to close the connection without ever completing the three-way handshake, while the ports that are closed reply with RST/ACK packets to the SYN requests.

The way to detect this attack is similar to the previous scan, where you will notice a lot of RST (**Expert Info**) or SYN/ACK packets without data transfers (**Conversations | TCP**) on the network.

Another indication is the short period of time under which these packets are sent (**Statistics | Flow Graph**).

Now, we will look at the **Flow Graph**, **Expert Info**, and **Conversations** windows in Wireshark for Stealth scan.

Wireshark's Flow Graph

While observing the TCP flow in the **Flow Graph**, we noted a sequence of SYN, SYN/ACK, and RSTs (indicating a half-open connection) along with SYN and RST/ACKs. Another indication is the fraction of seconds (displayed on the left-hand side) under which these packets are sent.

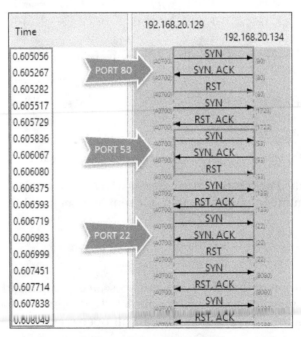

This diagram shows the half-open scan underway and how quickly the packets were sent under the "Time" column

Wireshark's Expert Info

The huge number of connection resets is another indication of a scan underway.

The Warning tab under Expert Info

Wireshark's Conversations

TCP Conversations also provide an insight to indicate that a half-open scan is underway, and the number of bytes associated with each attempt.

Address A	Port A	Address B	Port B	Packets	Bytes
192.168.20.129	63122	192.168.20.134	139	3	172
192.168.20.129	63122	192.168.20.134	445	3	172
192.168.20.129	63122	192.168.20.134	22	3	172
192.168.20.129	63122	192.168.20.134	53	3	172
192.168.20.129	6312?	192.168.20.134	25	3	172
192.168.20.129	6312? Open Ports		3306	3	172
192.168.20.129	6312z	192.168.2(134	23	3	172
192.168.20.129	63122	192.168.20.134	21	3	172
192.168.20.129	63122	192.168.20.134	80	3	172
192.168.20.129	63122	192.168.20.134	8180	3	172
192.168.20.129	63122	192.168.20.134	5432	3	172
192.168.20.129	63122	192.168.20.134	8009	3	172
192.168.20.129	6312?	192.168.2? 134	993	2	118
192.168.20.129	63? Closed Ports		1723	2	118
192.168.20.129	62?.	?4	554	2	118
192.168.20.129	63122	192.168.20.134	1720	2	118

The number of packets and bytes transferred for each Conversation

The number 3 in the Packets column indicates a SYN, SYN/ACK, and RST packets, and the number 2 indicates the SYN sent by Nmap and RST/ACK received for a closed port.

NULL scan

During a NULL scan, unusual TCP packets are sent with *no* flags set. If the resultant of this is *no response*, it means that the port is either open or filtered, while the RST/ACK response means that the port is closed.

A quick way to detect whether such a scan is underway is to filter on `tcp.flags == 0x00`.

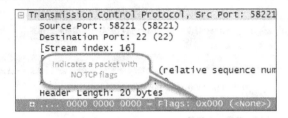

UDP scan

The last three techniques were related to the TCP-based scans. Many common protocols work over UDP as well (DNS, SNMP, TFTP, and so on) and scans are conducted to detect whether such ports are open or not.

No response to a UDP port scan indicates that the port is either open or firewalled, and a response of an ICMP `Destination Unreachable / Port Unreachable` means that the port is closed.

Detect UDP Scans by filtering on `(icmp.type == 3) && (icmp.code == 3)`.

ICMP Type 3 = Destination Unreachable

ICMP Code 3 = Port Unreachable

Other scanning attempts

The following scanning techniques go beyond the traditional port scanning techniques and help the attacker in the further enumeration of the network.

ACK scan

An ACK flag scan never locates an open port; rather, it only provides the result in the form of *filtered* or *unfiltered* and is generally used to detect the presence of a firewall.

No response means that the port is filtered, and the RST response indicates that the port is unfiltered.

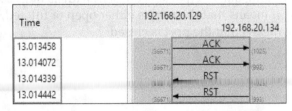

The Flow Graph (TCP) of an ACK flag scan

IP Protocol scan

An IP Protocol scan is conducted by attackers to determine the presence of additional IP protocols in use by the victim. For example, if a router is scanned using this technique, it might reveal the use of the other protocols , such as EGP, IGP, EIGRP, and so on.

No response indicates that a protocol is present or the response is filtered, while an ICMP `Destination Unreachable / Protocol Unreachable` indicates that the protocol is not supported by the device.

To detect this scan using Wireshark, we can filter the traffic based on: `(icmp.type == 3) && (icmp.code == 2)`.

```
ICMP Type 3 = Destination Unreachable
ICMP Code 2 = Protocol Unreachable
```

OS fingerprinting attempts

OS fingerprinting is the technique where an attacker tries to identify the operating system running on the target machine(s). An attacker can perform either passive or active fingerprinting.

In passive fingerprinting, an attacker monitors the traffic to and from a target machine and looks for certain indications, such as the initial IP TTL values, TCP window size, or a user-agent string, and other unique operating system characteristics to identify the OS in use. For example, a User-Agent string of Mozilla/5.0 (X11; Linux i686; rv:31.0) Gecko/20100101 Firefox/31.0 Iceweasel/31.5.0 helps the attacker assume that the target is running a Linux machine. However, user-agent strings and other factors can be modified using a number of tools. Hence, it is not a reliable method.

The tools required are P0f and Ettercap.

Active OS fingerprinting provides a more reliable result for the attacker, but the probes sent during this activity make it detectable by Wireshark and other advanced detection tools.

The following are different techniques that are used for OS fingerprinting:

- **ICMP-based fingerprinting:** Certain tools make use of unique ICMP probes to detect how an OS responds and make a guess based on that. The following are important filters for such a case:

  `(icmp.type == 8) && (!(icmp.code == 0))`

Some tools (for example, xprobe2) use ICMP Echo requests with an unusual ICMP code, so the preceding filter helps us detect those attempts.

`(icmp.type == 13) || (icmp.type == 15) || (icmp.type == 17)`

Other tools tend to send ICMP Timestamp requests (13), ICMP Information requests (15), and ICMP Address Mask requests (17) in order to perform OS fingerprinting.

- **TCP/IP-based fingerprinting**: Specific TCP probes with specific field values are sent and monitored for OS-based responses in order to detect the type of OS in use.

For example, one of the tests that are conducted is to send the TCP SYN packets and record the SYN/ACK responses in order to test the value of **Initial Sequence Number (ISN)**.

More details about such attempts can be found at `https://nmap.org/book/osdetect-methods.html`.

Laura Chappell shared an interesting *Sample Security Profile* at Sharkfest 2013. The profile includes coloring rules based on certain filters for different scanning, fingerprinting, and other illegal activities on the network. As of writing, this profile can be downloaded from `bit.ly/nmapcolors`.

Detect password cracking attempts

Password cracking is the process of making meaningful or random attempts at guessing the password. There are several techniques to do so. However, following are the two most popular ways to crack passwords.

- Brute-force attacks
- Dictionary-based attacks

Brute-force attacks

Brute-forcing is a method that tries a combination of numbers, lowercase and uppercase letters, and special characters to crack a password. This can be performed using certain tools such as Brutus, THC Hydra, Medusa, Burp Suite intruder, and many other tools available online. Brute-force attempts can be made on numerous services running on the network that involve authentication, such as FTP, SSH, POP3, HTTP, Telnet, RDP, and many more.

Identifying POP3 password cracking

In the following example, we see a captured attempt to brute-force POP3.

No.	Time	Source	Destination	Protocol	Info
	Filter: pop.request.command == PASS			Expression... Clear Apply Save	
30225	*REF*	192.168.10.1	192.168.10.132	POP	C: PASS eeeevw
30226	0.000422	192.168.10.1	192.168.10.132	POP	C: PASS eeeevW
30264	0.074131	192.168.10.1	192.168.10.132	POP	C: PASS eeeevy
30312	0.199417	192.168.10.1	192.168.10.132	POP	C: PASS eeeevY
30322	0.249480	192.168.10.1	192.168.10.132	POP	C: PASS eeeevb
30325	0.262069	192.168.10.1	192.168.10.132	POP	C: PASS eeeevB
30326	0.262111	192.168.10.1	192.168.10.132	POP	C: PASS eeeevv
30330	0.277704	192.168.10.1	192.168.10.132	POP	C: PASS eeeevV
30331	0.277711	192.168.10.1	192.168.10.132	POP	C: PASS eeeevK
30332	0.277711	192.168.10.1	192.168.10.132	POP	C: PASS eeeevk
30345	0.327554	192.168.10.1	192.168.10.132	POP	C: PASS eeeevx
30346	0.327642	192.168.10.1	192.168.10.132	POP	C: PASS eeeevX

In the preceding figure, we used a display filter (pop.request.command == PASS) to narrow down on the password attempts made to access the POP3 service and look at the filtered packets; it is visible that a brute-force attempt is under progress.

Another indication of these attempts is how quickly these attempts were made. It is not possible for a human being to make so many attempts in fraction of seconds as highlighted under the **Time** column, hence indicating the use of a password cracking tool.

HTTP basic authentication

It is common to find this type of authentication when a user tries to access any web-based management for devices such as wireless access points and routers. In one of the security assessments, I found a web portal to manage a Cisco **Adaptive Security Device Manage (ASDM)** device that had this type of authentication and could be easily brute-forced, as it did not have any lockout mechanism as well.

 For HTTP basic authentication, a point to note is that the credentials are Base-64 encoded and not sent in clear text as in FTP or POP3. However, Base-64 can be easily decoded, as we will see while solving the CTF challenge.

Dictionary-based attacks

In dictionary-based attacks, a limited set of words (wordlist) is used to crack passwords.

Detecting FTP password cracking

For the purpose of this demonstration, we used THC Hydra to crack FTP's password using a dictionary-based attack. The following is the trace file:

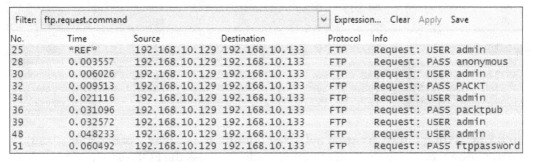

No.	Time	Source	Destination	Protocol	Info
25	*REF*	192.168.10.129	192.168.10.133	FTP	Request: USER admin
28	0.003557	192.168.10.129	192.168.10.133	FTP	Request: PASS anonymous
30	0.006026	192.168.10.129	192.168.10.133	FTP	Request: USER admin
32	0.009513	192.168.10.129	192.168.10.133	FTP	Request: PASS PACKT
34	0.021116	192.168.10.129	192.168.10.133	FTP	Request: USER admin
36	0.031096	192.168.10.129	192.168.10.133	FTP	Request: PASS packtpub
39	0.032572	192.168.10.129	192.168.10.133	FTP	Request: USER admin
48	0.048233	192.168.10.129	192.168.10.133	FTP	Request: USER admin
51	0.060492	192.168.10.129	192.168.10.133	FTP	Request: PASS ftppassword

The use of ftp.request.command to filter on FTP requests

In the preceding figure, we can notice random words being tried as password for the user `admin` indicating a wordlist-based attack under progress. Another indication is the fraction of seconds under which these passwords are attempted, which can be viewed under the **Time** column.

Just in case we needed to verify whether the attacker succeeded in those attempts, we can filter in on `ftp.response.code == 230` and see if there are any packets that match this filter.

Well, in the current scenario, we found one packet that matches our filtering rule. This indicates that the attack was successful and the attacker found the password for the user `msfadmin`.

 Another flag for detecting password cracking attempts is the humungous number of TCP conversations, which can be viewed under **Statistics**.

Miscellaneous attacks

In this section, we will look at some uncategorized but important attacks from a network's perspective.

FTP bounce attack

This is an old technique to perform port scanning in a stealthy way. The vulnerability lies in the PORT command used by FTP to transfer data in the ACTIVE mode.

Using this technique, an attacker can instruct the FTP server to open a connection to a particular port of a machine that might not be the originating client. Such a situation may allow an attacker to perform a port scan on a target by hiding his own identity. Nmap has an option -b to perform this type of scan. However, most of the FTP servers out there are aware about this attack and are configured accordingly to block such a scan and hence prevent an FTP bounce attack.

In a rare case, if you doubt that someone is trying to perform such an attack on the network, then you may want to use the following filters:

```
ftp.request.command == "PORT"
```

```
ftp.response.code == 226 || ftp.response.code == 426
```

```
Response Code of 226 means "Closing data connection. Requested file
action successful" and 426 means "Connection closed; transfer aborted".
Nmap uses these response codes to determine whether the port is open or
closed.
```

 More secure alternatives to FTP are available in the form of SFTP and SCP, which transfer data over an encrypted channel.

DNS zone transfer

By default, DNS uses UDP port 53 for normal queries and responses, and TCP port 53 for zone transfers and larger name queries and responses.

Capture filter for DNS-only traffic is tcp port 53 or udp port 53.

DNS zone transfer is a technique to replicate DNS databases across multiple DNS servers. It can be performed in the following two ways:

- Full/complete [AXFR]
- Incremental [IXFR]

An attacker might try to perform a zone transfer to know about the DNS database. You're not expected to see such traffic very frequently on the wire. From an attack perspective, we should look for complete zone transfer attempts, and the following filter can be useful in a scenario such as `dns.qry.type == 252`.

SSL stripping attack

Simply put, this attack forces the victim's browser to communicate over HTTP instead of HTTPS, and since the victim interacts over HTTP (a plain-text protocol), this makes it easy for the attacker to comprehend the communication.

> The inner workings of this attack are really interesting, and I highly recommend that you visit `http://www.thoughtcrime.org/software/sslstrip/` to understand the attack, download the Python script, and perform this attack in a test environment locally.

As mentioned, for the purpose of this attack, we will use **sslstrip** (written by Moxie Marlinspike). This tool also comes preinstalled in the current version of Kali Linux, a penetration testing Linux distribution, (`https://www.kali.org/`).

The following is an example of Gmail credentials captured in plain text after the successful execution of the attack:

```
⊞ Form item: "GALX" = "iLLGOCpBk_Q"
⊞ Form item: "continue" = "http://mail.google.com/mail/"
⊞ Form item: "service" = "mail"
⊞ Form item: "rm" = "false"
⊞ Form item: "ltmpl" = "default"
⊞ Form item: "scc" = "1"
⊞ Form item: "ss" = "1"
⊞ Form item: "osid" = "1"
⊞ Form item: "_utf8" = "▨"
⊞ Form item: "bgresponse" = "!FBdChXIXE5uStyNEA92AAJecXX
⊞ Form item: "pstMsg" = "1"
⊞ Form item: "dnConn" = ""
⊞ Form item: "checkConnection" = ""
⊞ Form item: "checkedDomains" = "youtube"
⊞ Form item: "Email" = "randomuser@gmail.com"
⊞ Form item: "Passwd" = "THE!R!SHC@FE"
⊞ Form item: "signIn" = "Sign in"
```

Gmail credentials in plain text

Next, we can see the Yahoo! mail credentials in plain text.

```
[Full request URI: http://login.yahoo.com/?.src=ym&.int
[HTTP request 1/2]
[Response in frame: 8522]
[Next request in frame: 8525]
HTML Form URL Encoded: application/x-www-form-urlencoded
⊞ Form item: "countrycode" = "1"
⊞ Form item: "username" = "randomuser@yahoo.com"
⊞ Form item: "passwd" = "SUPER$3CR3TP@$$w0rd"
```

Yahoo! Mail credentials in plain text

Complementary tools to Wireshark

In this section, we will look at some fantastic tools that complement Wireshark and help us in performing better analysis.

Xplico

Xplico is a fantastic open source network forensics analysis tool and comes packaged with popular pen-testing and forensics Linux distributions.

Up and running with Xplico on Kali Linux:

1. To install Xplico manually, run the following command:

    ```
    sudo apt-get install xplico
    ```

2. Once installed, we need to start Xplico's service by running:

    ```
    /etc/init.d/xplico start
    ```

3. Also, make sure that the web service is running. This can be done by running `/etc/init.d/apache2 start`. Now we need to open the browser and browse `http://127.0.0.1:9876` and use `xplico` and `xplico` as the username and password.

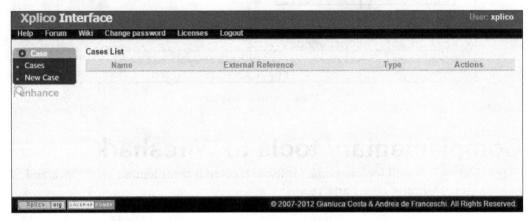

Xplico's GUI post-login

4. First, we need to create a new case and then a new session inside that case and later upload the PCAP file for analysis.

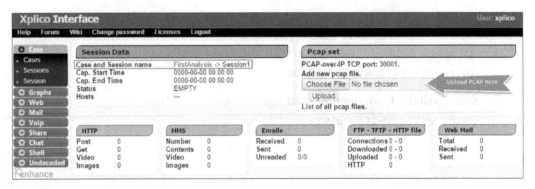

As mentioned in its Wiki page, Xplico can help reconstruct the contents of acquisitions performed with a packet sniffer.

Sysdig

This is an awesome tool for people performing troubleshooting activities and complements Wireshark very well. Sysdig makes system-level troubleshooting less of a pain and more fun. Sysdig can create trace files with the -w command-line flag and read them using the -r flag, as shown in the following screenshot:

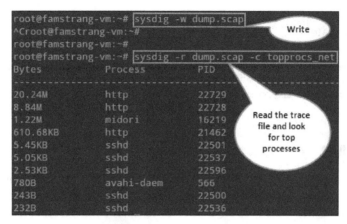

Writing and reading a trace file using Sysdig

Sysdig also includes a set of helpful scripts, also known as chisels in its terminology, which can be used with the -c flag. To look at the available list of chisels with Sysdig's use, see the -cl flag, as follows:

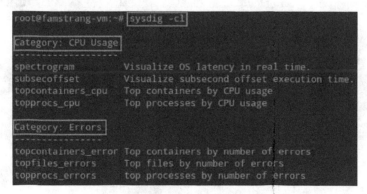

The list of chisels in Sysdig

We can also create our own chisels to work with Sysdig. Currently, Sysdig has categorized its chisels into nine categories as mentioned here:

- CPU usage
- Errors

- I/O
- Logs
- Miscellaneous
- Network
- Performance
- Security
- System state

 To dive in-depth with Sysdig, I recommend going over to `http://www.sysdig.org/` and getting hands-on practice with this tool.

Pcap2XML

Pcap2XML is a handy utility, which is used to parse 802.11 packets at a macro-level. It converts the capture file(s) into the equivalent XML and SQLite files, and then later perform XPath, XQuery, and/or SQL queries to derive macro-stats from them.

This tool complements Wireshark by offering the features that are currently not present in Wireshark. For example, we can use this utility to parse out the unique MAC addresses in an 802.11 capture file.

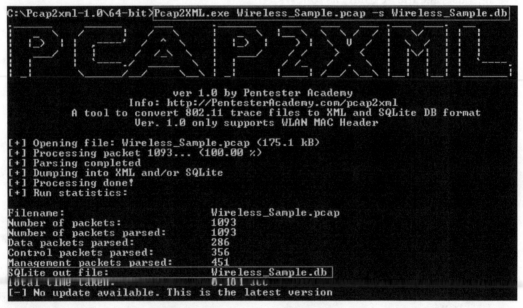

Converting a PCAP into DB file using Pcap2XML

After converting the capture file into a database file, we can open it with any software that is used to edit database files compatible with SQLite, and perform the SQL queries to get the desired result.

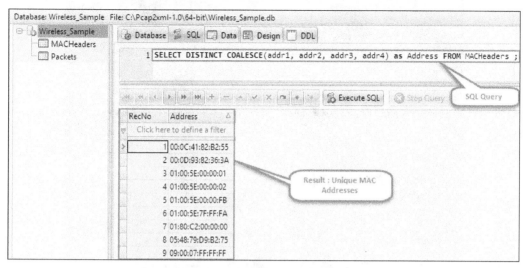

SQL query executed on the DB file

We can also run XPath queries after converting the PCAP file to an XML file using –x option with Pcap2XML.

Pcap2XML can be downloaded from
https://github.com/securitytube/pcap2xml.

SSHFlow

SSHFlow is an interesting and "work-under-progress" utility written by Alex Weber to examine the PCAP files for SSH traffic. It is written in Python and works by guessing what is being tunneled across an SSH session based on the most common packet sizes.

The current features of the utility include the detection of the following:

- File transfers
- Interactive sessions
- Nested tunnels
- X11 forwarding

The following is an example usage of SSHFlow. This screenshot, reflects a user interacting with a remote machine via SSH.

```
                    # ./sshflow.py SSH.pcap
| sshflow
loading analyzers
  general_stats
  nested_tunnels
  interactive_session
  jabber
  x11_tunneling
  scp
generating statistics from pcap file, please wait...
  SSH handshake: 192.168.20.129:56467 -> 192.168.20.134:22

processed 390 packets, analysis follows...

--- analysis of conversation: 192.168.20.129:56467 -> 192.168.20.134:22 ---
General statistics
  Detected ciphersuite: aes128-ctr hmac-md5 zlib@openssh.com
  Smallest possible packet for ciphersuite: 48
  Packets sent by client: 111
  Packets sent by server: 136
  Average client packet length: 890
  Average server packet length: 1185
  Total bytes (of SSH data) sent by client: 7120
  Total bytes (of SSH data) sent by server: 15416
  Most common client packet size: [(48, 101), (64, 3), (144, 2), (32, 1), (16, 1)]
  Most common server packet size: [(48, 57), (64, 48), (80, 15), (112, 3), (1448, 3)]
  Average time between client packets: 0.618071027236
  Average time between server packets: 0.507311671527

-> Likely an interactive shell session
--- End of analysis ---
```

An interactive session detected in the SSH.pcap file

The following screenshot, shows a file copy in action:

```
                    # ./sshflow.py SSH2.pcap
| sshflow
loading analyzers
  general_stats
  nested_tunnels
  interactive_session
  jabber
  x11_tunneling
  scp
generating statistics from pcap file, please wait...
  SSH handshake: 192.168.10.129:39961 -> 192.168.10.133:22

processed 148 packets, analysis follows...

--- analysis of conversation: 192.168.10.129:39961 -> 192.168.10.133:22 ---
General statistics
  Detected ciphersuite: aes128-ctr hmac-md5 zlib@openssh.com
  Smallest possible packet for ciphersuite: 48
  Packets sent by client: 69
  Packets sent by server: 12
  Average client packet length: 7149
  Average server packet length: 275
  Total bytes (of SSH data) sent by client: 78640
  Total bytes (of SSH data) sent by server: 2200
  Most common client packet size: [(1448, 51), (64, 4), (504, 4), (32, 2), (144, 2)]
  Most common server packet size: [(48, 5), (32, 1), (64, 1), (80, 1), (128, 1)]
  Average time between client packets: 0.0535690151155
  Average time between server packets: 0.91129709994
-> Likely a file copy from client to server
--- End of analysis ---
```

The file transfer detected in the SSH2.pcap file

[You can find out more about SSHFlow at
`https://github.com/alexwebr/sshflow`.]

Important display filters

In this section, we will look at some display filters which will come handy in day-to-day protocol analysis with regard to security.

Filters based on protocols

In this section, we will look at some of the most useful display filters for the more common protocols.

DNS

The commonly used display filters for DNS are as follows:

`dns`

`dns.query.response == 0`

`dns.query.response == 1`

`dns.flags.rcode == 2 [Server Failure]`

FTP

Some of the common display filters that can be used while traversing FTP communication are as follows:

1. `ftp.request.command == "USER"`: This filter is used to filter data based on a specific FTP command. A list of FTP commands can be found at `http://en.wikipedia.org/wiki/List_of_FTP_commands`.

2. `ftp.request.arg == "anonymous"`: We may use this filter to narrow down on the precise arguments passed to the FTP commands.

3. `ftp.response.code == 530`: Filtering for specific FTP response codes can help us identify any specific issues on the network. For example, if we see a lot of 530 response codes in FTP traffic, there is a high chance that someone is attempting to crack passwords.

4. `ftp || ftp-data (command control and data transfer)`: This filter allows us to view complete FTP traffic on the wire including the commands and data being transferred over the wire.

HTTP

The following are relevant display filters available in Wireshark for HTTP or HTTP/2 traffic:

`http`

`http2`

`http.set_cookie`

`http.cookie`

`http.request.method`

`http.response.code >=300 and http.response.code <400 [Redirections]`

`http.response.code >=400 and http.response.code <500 [Client-Side Errors]`

`http.response.code >500 [Server-Side Errors]`

`http.user_agent [Malwares might try to beacon using some specific User-Agent String, or Scanners/Tools can be identified using a particular User-Agent String]`

The following is an example of popular automated SQL injection tools detected by Wireshark based on the user-agent strings:

- Havij (an automated SQL injection tool) in action is shown in the following screenshot:

```
GET /sqli-labs/Less-1/?id=1 HTTP/1.1\r\n
Host: 192.168.20.129\r\n
Accept: */*\r\n
User-Agent: Mozilla/4.0 (compatible; MSIE 7.0; Windows NT 5.1; SV1; .NET CLR 2.0.50727) Havij\r\n
Connection: Close\r\n
```

- Sqlmap (an automated SQL injection tool) in action is shown in the following screenshot:

```
GET /sqli-labs/Less-1/?id=1 HTTP/1.1\r\n
Accept-Language: en-us,en;q=0.5\r\n
Accept-Encoding: gzip,deflate\r\n
Host: 127.0.0.1\r\n
Accept: text/html,application/xhtml+xml,application/xml;q=0.9,*/*;q=0.8\r\n
User-Agent: sqlmap/1.0-dev-nongit-20150228 (http://sqlmap.org)\r\n
```

The following command can help to filter out malicious or abnormal hostname traffic. For example, when a malware performs a phone-home mechanism.

`http.host matches "some-domain-name"`

Filters based on unique signatures and regular expressions

Unique signatures: We may also choose to filter on unique signatures for different file types out there. For example, when looking for a ZIP file in the trace file, we can use the following display filter:

`frame contains "\x50\x4B\x03\x04"`

\x50\x4B\x03\x04 is the unique signature for the ZIP file. These signatures are sometimes referred to as magic numbers. The following table highlights these signatures for some common file extensions and can be used with `contains` keyword in the display filter.

The sample usage of these signatures can be made as:

Syntax: `frame contains "<Signature>"`

Example: `frame contains "\x25\x50\x44\x46"` (for PDF file(s))

These can be handy during an analysis.

> A comprehensive list of file signatures can be found at
> `http://en.wikipedia.org/wiki/List_of_file_signatures`.

Regular expressions

Wireshark offers us another neat feature: to use **Regular Expressions (RegEx)** with our display filters. To use RegEx with display filters we use `matches` keyword. The following are some examples:

1. To locate any keywords (`password`, `confidential`, or `secret`) in the trace file, use the following filter:

   `frame matches "(?i)(password|confidential|secret)"`

2. To look for any `.com` domain(s) in the HTTP traffic, use the following filter:

   `http matches "[a-zA-Z0-9\-\.]+\.(?i)(com)"`

3. To find any email addresses in an SMTP traffic, use the following filter:

   `smtp matches "[a-zA-Z0-9._%+-]+@[a-zA-Z0-9._%+-]"`

By making use of regular expressions, we can search for popular text in the string fields and byte sequences. The better we are with RegEx, the faster we can traverse though a trace file and improve our analysis time.

 Regular expressions in Wireshark use the **Perl Compatible Regular Expression** (PCRE).

Learn more about RegEx at http://regexone.com/.

Nailing the CTF challenge

The CTF events are common contents at security conferences worldwide. In some CTF challenges, we are given a PCAP file that needs to be analyzed to solve a particular challenge or generally get the flag. This is exactly what we will be doing next. We will solve the CTF challenge given in the **Hack3rCon 3** (http://hack3rcon.org/) conference.

Challenge: Capture the flag in the given PCAP file. This file can be downloaded from http://sickbits.net/other/hc3.pcap-04.cap.

Solution: We will solve this challenge using Wireshark and introduce some other utilities, which will help solve it. The steps are as follows:

1. Open the PCAP file with Wireshark and see the protocols in action.

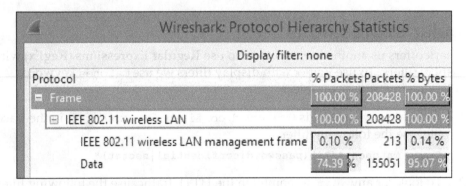

2. We can see that this file contains 802.11 frames. The next step would be to identify the security algorithm in use, to see if we can crack the encrypted 802.11 frames and actually see what is going on behind the scenes. We can do this by filtering on unique signatures in each type of security algorithms, namely, WEP, WPA, and WPA2.

We can use **IV (Initialization Vector)**, a random number used along with a secret key for data encryption, to identify whether WEP is in use or not. Hence, filtering on `wlan.wep.iv` will display any WEP-encrypted traffic in the trace file.

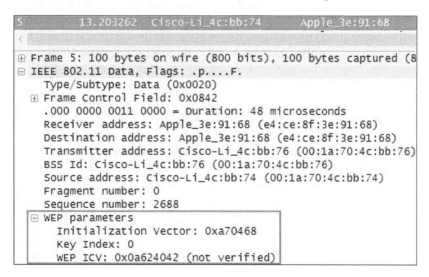

Shows 74.4 percent of the total packets based on the filter

In the preceding image, we note 155051 packets that match our filter, and if we look further into frame 5, we can see the following:

```
5        13.203262   Cisco-Li_4c:bb:74        Apple_3e:91:68
<
⊞ Frame 5: 100 bytes on wire (800 bits), 100 bytes captured (8
⊟ IEEE 802.11 Data, Flags: .p....F.
    Type/Subtype: Data (0x0020)
  ⊞ Frame Control Field: 0x0842
    .000 0000 0011 0000 = Duration: 48 microseconds
    Receiver address: Apple_3e:91:68 (e4:ce:8f:3e:91:68)
    Destination address: Apple_3e:91:68 (e4:ce:8f:3e:91:68)
    Transmitter address: Cisco-Li_4c:bb:76 (00:1a:70:4c:bb:76)
    BSS Id: Cisco-Li_4c:bb:76 (00:1a:70:4c:bb:76)
    Source address: Cisco-Li_4c:bb:74 (00:1a:70:4c:bb:74)
    Fragment number: 0
    Sequence number: 2688
  ⊟ WEP parameters
      Initialization Vector: 0xa70468
      Key Index: 0
      WEP ICV: 0x0a624042 (not verified)
```

Hence, for the time being, we may assume that WEP is used for encrypting this 802.11 traffic.

3. WEP is a weak algorithm with numerous weaknesses, and we can attempt to crack it. However, to crack WEP, we need to have a minimum number of IVs captured, and if we notice in the screenshot that shows 74.4 percent of the total packets based on the filter, we have 155051 frames containing IV, which is enough to attempt to crack the WEP key.

    To crack WEP, we will make use of a popular and fantastic utility named `aircrack-ng`. The command used to crack WEP in this case is `aircrack-ng hc3.pcap-04.cap`.

```
                            Aircrack-ng 1.2 rc2


                 [00:00:00] Tested 861 keys (got 50459 IVs)

    KB    depth    byte(vote)
    0     0/ 13    28(63744) A8(60928) 86(58880) C7(58880) 3D(58624)
    1     0/  1    57(76544) 0F(60928) 34(59392) 5B(58880) D4(57856)
    2     1/  2    1E(61952) A8(59648) 67(59136) 03(58624) 5F(58368)
    3     0/  1    B4(75264) 31(61184) 7F(60416) 66(58112) 83(57856)
    4     9/  4    F9(58368) 07(57856) EF(57856) FF(57856) 3B(57600)

             KEY FOUND! [ 28:E6:6B:E9:D3:B6:20:95:DD:E9:2F:BE:37 ]
          Decrypted correctly: 100%
```

Successfully cracked WEP

4. Now, we may use the `airdecap-ng` to decrypt the frames in the PCAP file using that key, or we can add the decryption key to Wireshark by removing the colons (:) in the key found. Let us do this using Wireshark.

Check the wireless toolbar and select "Decryption Keys...' option from the wireless toolbar

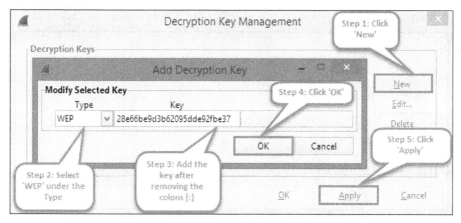

Steps to add WEP decryption key to Wireshark

5. After adding the decryption key to Wireshark, select **Wireshark** from the drop-down menu highlighted in the Wireless toolbar and click on ⟳ (**Reload** button) on the main toolbar, to reload the trace file. Once reloaded, we can see a mix of 802.11 traffic and other protocols, such as ICMP and ARP. To get rid of the 802.11 traffic, use the display filter: `llc` and then we will be presented with some interesting traffic that can be analyzed.

    At this point, we can select to export these packets into a separate PCAP file [recommended] or just work with this.

6. After going over to **Statistics | Conversations** and then to the **TCP** tab, we can see conversations over FTP, SMTP, and POP3.

Interesting conversation

After following the TCP stream on the highlighted conversation, we were able to note the file signature for a ZIP file; hence, we saved it as a ZIP file using the **Save As** button as follows:

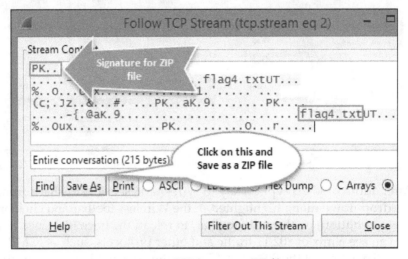

Saving the TCP Stream as a ZIP file

We also see an interesting keyword in the TCP stream, as highlighted in the preceding image, and hence chose to save this file as `flag.zip`.

1. We are still not finished because this ZIP file turns out to be password-protected as follows:

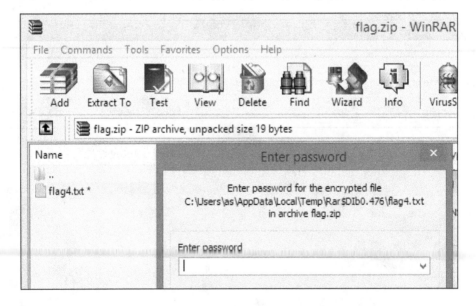

2. Let's get back to our PCAP and see if we missed anything. Navigating further into the trace, we notice SMTP and POP3 communication. If we move and expand on **frame 105840**, we will note the use of **Internet Message Format (IMF)** and expanding on this frame reflects Base-64 encoded string as shown in the following screenshot:

```
☐ Internet Message Format
      Received: from [192.168.0.122] ([2.2.2.1]) by c
      Message-ID: <4F9DB1BE.9060902@carolinacon8.com>
      Date: Sun, 29 Apr 2012 17:25:18 -0400
   ⊞ From: metalman <metalman@carolinacon8.com>, 1 i
      User-Agent: Mozilla/5.0 (Windows; U; windows NT
      MIME-version: 1.0
   ⊞ To: crashman@carolinacon8.com, metalman@carolin
      Subject: yo...
   ⊞ Content-Type: text/plain; charset=ISO-8859-1; f
      Content-Transfer-Encoding: 7bit
      Return-Path: <metalman@carolinacon8.c
   ☐ Line-based text data: text/plain                Base-64
         cm,\r\n                                        encoded
            is this right?\r\n                          string
         \r\n
      dGhlIHBhc3N3b3JkIGlzIGJvc3Rvbk1BMTk3Nwo=\r\n
```

3. Base-64, in and of itself, can be easily decoded using a number of tools and online resources. The following is a screenshot that reflects the decoded Base-64 string.

```
                 :~# python
Python 2.7.3 (default, Mar 14 2014, 11:57:14)
[GCC 4.7.2] on linux2
Type "help", "copyright", "credits" or "licen
>>> import base64
>>> base64.b64decode("dGhlIHBhc3N3b3JkIGlzIGJ
'the password is bostonMA1977\n'
```

Congratulations!

We were able to open the password-protected ZIP file by using the decoded password bostonMA1977. The following is our flag for the challenge:

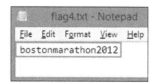

FLAG is highlighted in the image

Summary

In this chapter, we looked at the most common attacks that can occur in a LAN environment and saw how we can use Wireshark's optimum features to detect such attacks. Also, we need to emphasize on baselining for good traffic, in order to better deal with the threats to LAN security, so that any anomaly thereof can be easily detected via Wireshark. Another handy trick is to possess a good list of filters and coloring rules to match them and save the analysis time. We took a brief look at the tools that complement Wireshark very well and used some to solve the CTF challenge at the end.

4
Probing E-mail Communications

Messages have been exchanged since centuries; however, the means to exchange these messages have evolved, and privacy has become a bigger and more important concern than ever before. From the time when messengers were used to deliver messages physically to the recent times when the Internet is used to deliver messages, the vulnerabilities have existed and are not completely fixed, even today. In this chapter, we will look at a contemporary way of messaging, that is e-mails, and the security threats it brings to the table.

In this chapter we will learn the following:

- How to use Wireshark to detect numerous attacks on SMTP
- Solve SMTP forensics challenges using Wireshark and a bit of Python
- Important filters to detect unusual SMTP traffic

In the 1960s, we were introduced to electronic mail (e-mail), and since then it has become the de facto standard to exchange messages over the Internet whether casually or professionally. The protocols used in such communications are SMTP, POP3, and IMAP. Inherently, these protocols transfer data over clear-text, which as we have seen in the previous chapter can be easily intercepted on the network.

In a rather simple scenario, e-mail communications use SMTP (TCP/25) or submission (TCP/587), also known as push protocol, to send e-mails, and they may use any of POP3 (TCP/110) or IMAP (TCP/143), also known as pull protocol(s), to receive e-mails on an e-mail client such as Outlook. We may choose to run these over secure channel such as TLS as well, for example SMTP's (TCP/465), POP3's (TCP/995), and IMAP's (TCP/993).

Most of the organizations these days have an anti-spam mechanism integrated into their security devices, which tend to offer real-time spam protection from zero-day threats and blended attacks involving malware, botnets, phishing, and so on. However, there may be times when such solutions may incorrectly identify legitimate e-mails as spam (false-positive) or allow a spam e-mail (false-negative). In such scenarios, if a capture is running on the network, then Wireshark can be used to probe such communications.

Assuming that you know how the e-mail communication works, we will begin with some intriguing challenges available online and solve them, using Wireshark.

E-mail forensics challenges

In this section, we will analyze the trace file(s) in order to solve the challenges. The trace files contain interesting e-mail traffic, waiting for analysis. Let's dive in.

Challenge 1 – Normal login session

Description: A user logs in to the mail server to access his e-mail.

> Required files for this challenge are available at
> http://securityoverride.org/challenges/forensics/3/.

Goal: Identify the username and password from the given trace file.

Analysis: Key points about the trace file available with this challenge are:

- **ESMTP (Extended SMTP)**: This can be seen in this trace file. ESMTP extends the SMTP protocol by providing extensions.
- **SMTP-AUTH**: This extension is used in this trace for authentication purpose.
- **AUTH LOGIN**: This command in packet 8 of this trace is used to make an authenticated login to the server. After AUTH LOGIN command has been sent to the server, the server asks for the username and password by sending Base64-encoded text (questions) to the client.

No.	Time	Source	Destination	Protocol	Length	Info
1	0.000000	192.168.0.3	192.168.0.1	TCP	62	1077→25 [SYN] Seq=0 Win=16384 Len=0 MS
2	0.000000	192.168.0.1	192.168.0.3	TCP	62	25→1077 [SYN, ACK] Seq=0 Ack=1 Win=175
3	0.020029	192.168.0.3	192.168.0.1	TCP	60	1077→25 [ACK] Seq=1 Ack=1 Win=17520 Le
4	0.020029	192.168.0.1	192.168.0.3	SMTP	158	S: 220 Server Microsoft ESMTP MAIL Ser
5	0.030043	192.168.0.3	192.168.0.1	SMTP	67	C: EHLO client
6	0.190274	192.168.0.1	192.168.0.3	TCP	54	25→1077 [ACK] Seq=105 Ack=14 Win=17507
7	0.420605	192.168.0.1	192.168.0.3	SMTP	290	S: 250 Server Hello [192.168.0.3] | 25
8	0.430619	192.168.0.3	192.168.0.1	SMTP	66	C: AUTH LOGIN
9	0.430619	192.168.0.1	192.168.0.3	SMTP	72	S: 334 VXNlcm5hbwU6
10	0.430619	192.168.0.3	192.168.0.1	SMTP	64	C: User: QXVkaQ==
11	0.430619	192.168.0.1	192.168.0.3	SMTP	72	S: 334 UGFzc3dvcmQ6
12	0.430619	192.168.0.3	192.168.0.1	SMTP	64	C: Pass: MTIzNGFk
13	0.440634	192.168.0.1	192.168.0.3	SMTP	91	S: 235 2.7.0 Authentication successful

Authentication process shows credentials encoded as Base64

 Base64 is an encoding (different from encryption) scheme designed to allow representation of binary data as ASCII text, by translating it into a radix-64 representation. Base64 can easily be decoded and is not recommended to be use for confidential information.

Base64 decoding for this trace can be done in Wireshark, by simply following the steps mentioned in the following screenshot:

Source	Destination	Protocol	Length	Info
192.1	Mark Packet (toggle)	SMTP	66	C: AUTH LOGIN **1**
192.1	Ignore Packet (toggle)	SMTP	72	S: 33 **Right-click any SMTP Frame**
192.1	Set Time Reference (toggle)	SMTP	64	C: Us...
192.1	Time Shift...	SMTP	72	S: 334 UGFzc3dvcmQ6
192.1	Edit Packet	SMTP	64	C: Pass: MTIzNGFk
192.1	Packet Comment...	SMTP	91	S: 235 2.7.0 Authenticatio
192.1		SMTP	94	C: MAIL FROM: <Audi@securi
192.1	Manually Resolve Address	SMTP	104	S: 250 2.1.0 Audi@security
192.1	Apply as Filter ▸	SMTP	79	C: RCPT TO: <Gotya@i.suck>
192.1	Prepare a Filter ▸	SMTP	79	S: 250 2.1.5 Gotya@i.suck
192.1	Conversation Filter ▸	SMTP	60	C: DATA
192.1	Colorize Conversation ▸	SMTP	100	S: 354 Start mail input; e
192.1	SCTP ▸	SMTP	1404	C: DATA fragment, 1350 byt
192.1	Follow TCP Stream	TCP	54	25→1077 [ACK] Seq=535 Ack=
192.1	Follow UDP Stream	IMF	60	from: "Audi" <Audi@securit
192.1	Follow SSL Stream	SMTP	131	S: 250 2.6.0 <000801cad7e
192.1	Copy ▸	SMTP	60	C: QUIT
192.1		SMTP	109	S: 221 2.0.0 Server Servic

Protocol Preferences ▸ — Simple Mail Transfer Protocol Preferences...
Decode As... **2**
Print...
Show Packet in New Window

✓ Reassemble SMTP command and response lines spanning multiple TCP segments
✓ Reassemble SMTP DATA commands spanning multiple TCP segments
Decrypt AUTH parameters **3**

bytes on wire (528 bits), 6

Another way to decode Base64 is using any tool such as Burp Suite (which does rather more complex tasks than simply decoding Base64); online resources are available at `https://www.base64decode.org/`.

For the coders among us, we may also choose to script this out in Python. The following is a sample Python script written on Linux to decode Base64:

```
#!/usr/bin/python

import sys, base64

try:
    decodedResult = base64.b64decode(sys.argv[1])
    print("Base64 decoded value = " + decodedResult)

except:
    print("Please enter a valid Base64 encoded string, and TRY AGAIN
!")

#END
```

This code simply takes a Base64 encoded string as an input and returns the decoded value as follows:

```
               :~# python b64decoder.py QXVkaQ==
Base64 decoded value = Audi
               :~# python b64decoder.py MTIzNGFk
Base64 decoded value = 1234ad
```

The final solution is as shown in the following table:

Item	Base64 Encoded	Base64 Decoded
Username	QXVkaQ==	Audi
Password	MTIzNGFk	1234ad

Challenge 2 – Corporate espionage

Description: A spy manages to copy the image of the prototype of a car from one of the internal systems of an automobile firm. She understands that e-mail content can be sniffed and therefore pastes the image in a file and sends this file as an attachment. In this challenge we are provided with a trace file named Dhakkan.cap, which contains the packets captured while the espionage activity was under process.

Required files for this challenge are available at
`http://securityoverride.org/challenges/forensics/9/`.

Goal: Analyze and extract the image from the attachment and submit the following details:

- MD5 of the image
- Meeting place
- Date

Analysis: After a brief overview of the packets, we understand that the trace file contains SMTP traffic including a number of DATA commands.

A practical approach in such a situation is to look at the **TCP Conversations** and sort the conversations based on **Bytes**. After selecting the conversation with maximum number of bytes, click on **Follow Stream** to open that TCP stream.

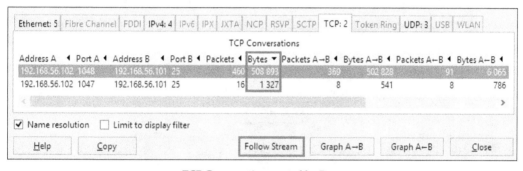

TCP Conversations sorted by Bytes

After inspecting the TCP stream, we deduce the following:

- **E-mail sender**: Dhakkan@securityoverride.com
- **E-mail recipient**: hacku@dhakkansecurity.com
- **Subject**: The secret Concept Car Photo
- **Content-Transfer-Encoding**: quoted-printable

- **Attachment name and format**: `secret.rtf` (Rich Text Format)

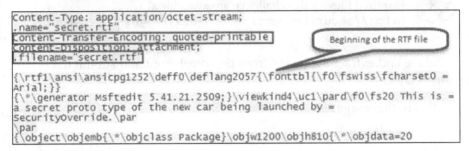

```
Content-Type: application/octet-stream;
.name="secret.rtf"
Content-Transfer-Encoding: quoted-printable        Beginning of the RTF file
Content-Disposition: attachment;
.filename="secret.rtf"
{\rtf1\ansi\ansicpg1252\deff0\deflang2057{\fonttbl{\f0\fswiss\fcharset0 =
Arial;}}
{\*\generator Msftedit 5.41.21.2509;}\viewkind4\uc1\pard\f0\fs20 This is =
a secret proto type of the new car being launched by =
SecurityOverride.\par
\par
{\object\objemb{\*\objclass Package}\objw1200\objh810{\*\objdata=20
```

TCP stream

Now, as we can see from the gathered information, the e-mail is encoded in quotable-printable format, and the attachment is in rtf format.

1. Extract the attachment from the provided trace file. Copy the RTF content from the stream and decode it as per the encoding scheme. Begin copying from the *beginning of the RTF file* as highlighted in the following screenshot and finish it.

The preceding image also reflects the **Location** and **date** details as asked in the challenge. Good catch.

Another way to extract e-mail attachments is as follows:

Use `imf` as the display filter and head to the packet details pane for the selected IMF packet.

Expand the **Internet Message Format** header and follow expansions to **Media type**, right-click and **Export Selected Packet Bytes**, and this export will lead to the extraction of the attached file.

2. Once the attachment is extracted from the trace file, we will need to decode the RTF content, which was copied from the TCP stream.

Following is a small Python script I wrote on Linux for the purpose of decoding:

```
#!/usr/bin/python

import os, quopri

encodedFile=open('/home/piyush/secret.rtf')
decodedFile=open('/home/piyush/decoded_secret.rtf', 'wb')

quopri.decode(encodedFile, decodedFile)

#END
```

No we will have a quick walkthrough of code. The code first imports the following two modules:

○   os to read from and write to file

○   quopri to decode quoted-printable encoding scheme

Then, the encodedFile variable stores the file object returned by the open() function. In this case, it opens secret.rtf, which we want to decode.

The next line of code creates a file object named decodedFile and creates a new file decoded_secret.rtf and opens it to write in a binary mode (wb).

Finally, we use the quopri.decode() function available in the quopri module to read from the encodedFile file object, that is, read the secret.rtf file and decode it. The decoded output is written to the decodedFile file object, that is, written to the decoded_secret.rtf.

An online resource to decode quoted-printable encoding is as follows: `http://www.motobit.com/util/quoted-printable-decoder.asp`.

Please feel free to select any resource as long as you're able to decode it.

3. Once decoded, open `decoded_secret.rtf` using WordPad as shown in the following figure:

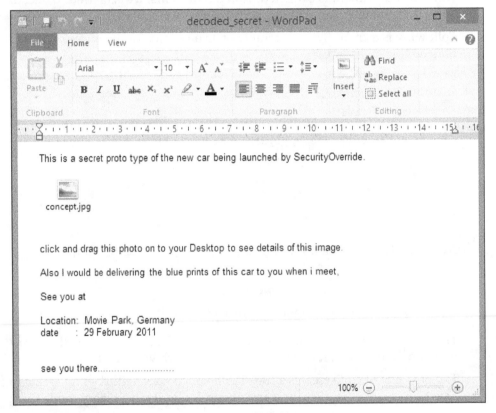

A decoded RTF file

In the last few steps, we extracted and decoded the attachment from the given trace file by using Wireshark and a Python script.

Now, in order to solve the challenge, we ought to extract the `content.jpg` file from the RTF file and create an MD5 hash of that image. To solve this final piece of the puzzle, we can drag and drop the `content.jpg` to a folder or desktop and then create its MD5 using software as **HashCalc** or a Linux utility, **md5sum**, as shown here:

```
                    :~# md5sum concept.jpg
3796102e17ff50382cb48160b76a3946   concept.jpg
```

The final solution is as follows:

- **MD5 of the image**: *3796102e17ff50382cb48160b76a3946*
- **Meeting place**: *Movie Park, Germany*
- **Date**: *29 February 2011*

Analyzing attacks on e-mail communications

E-mail communications can be tampered with to send spam messages and fake e-mails from important mail accounts, and even the recent Shellshock vulnerability can be exploited.

The users on an SMTP server can be enumerated by using the `EXPN`, `VRFY`, or `RCPT` commands. This can be achieved either manually by simply connecting to the SMTP server over port 25 and running the respective commands as shown in the following screenshot, or automatically via tools such as Nmap and Metasploit, which are discussed further in this section.

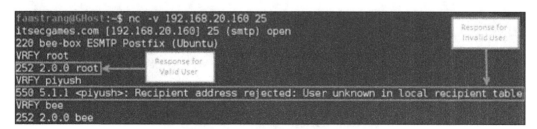

Manual SMTP enumeration using VRFY command

Detecting SMTP enumeration

To detect any SMTP enumeration attempts, we need to look for the following indications:

- A lot of VRFY or EXPN commands in the trace file

- Packets containing MAIL and RCPT commands with very less or no DATA commands

- A significant number of packets containing SMTP response code of 550

- Bunch of RSET commands

Using auxiliary module in Metasploit

Metasploit contains an auxiliary module named smtp_enum. This module uses a dictionary to perform username enumeration, and after successful execution of this module, we were able to verify that it works by sending a number of RCPT commands in order to do so.

```
msf auxiliary(smtp_enum) > run

[*] 192.168.20.160:25 Banner: 220 bee-box ESMTP Postfix (Ubuntu)
[+] 192.168.20.160:25 Users found: , avahi, avahi-autoipd, backup, bin, daemon,
ftp, games, gdm, gnats, haldaemon, hplip, irc, libuuid, list, lp, mail, man, mes
sagebus, news, nobody, postmaster, proxy, pulse, sshd, sync, sys, syslog, uucp,
www-data
```

User enumeration results from Metasploit's auxiliary module

The following is the filtered traffic of the user enumeration by Metasploit's auxiliary module.

No.	Source	Destination	Protocol	Info
15	192.168.20.140	192.168.20.160	SMTP	C: RCPT TO: bRZjrzFW@bee-box
21	192.168.20.140	192.168.20.160	SMTP	C: RCPT TO: @bee-box
27	192.168.20.140	192.168.20.160	SMTP	C: RCPT TO: 4Dgifts@bee-box
33	192.168.20.140	192.168.20.160	SMTP	C: RCPT TO: EZsetup@bee-box
39	192.168.20.140	192.168.20.160	SMTP	C: RCPT TO: OutOfBox@bee-box
45	192.168.20.140	192.168.20.160	SMTP	C: RCPT TO: adm@bee-box
51	192.168.20.140	192.168.20.160	SMTP	C: RCPT TO: admin@bee-box
57	192.168.20.140	192.168.20.160	SMTP	C: RCPT TO: administrator@bee-box
63	192.168.20.140	192.168.20.160	SMTP	C: RCPT TO: anon@bee-box
69	192.168.20.140	192.168.20.160	SMTP	C: RCPT TO: auditor@bee-box
77	192.168.20.140	192.168.20.160	SMTP	C: RCPT TO: avahi@bee-box
86	192.168.20.140	192.168.20.160	SMTP	C: RCPT TO: avahi-autoipd@bee-box
95	192.168.20.140	192.168.20.160	SMTP	C: RCPT TO: backup@bee-box
104	192.168.20.140	192.168.20.160	SMTP	C: RCPT TO: bbs@bee-box

Filter: smtp.req.command == "RCPT"

The filtered Wireshark capture of the mentioned attack

Display filters to identify SMTP enumeration:

```
smtp.req.command == "VRFY" || smtp.req.command == "EXPN"
smtp.req.command == "RCPT"
smtp.response.code == 550
//Indicates Requested action not taken: mailbox unavailable
smtp.req.command == "RSET"
```

Analyzing SMTP relay attack

SMTP relay attacks are used by attackers to send spam and malwares disguising under an authentic SMTP server. Popular tools, such as Metasploit and Nmap, can be used to verify if a mail server allows open relays or not, or else it can be performed manually as well. In the following example, Wireshark is used to analyze an open relay attack attempt by Nmap.

Filter:	smtp.response.code == 554			▾	Expression... Clear Apply Save	
No.	Source	Destination	Protocol	Info		
21	192.168.20.141	192.168.20.140	SMTP	S: 554 5.7.1 <relaytest@nmap.scanme.org>: Relay access denied		
27	192.168.20.141	192.168.20.140	SMTP	S: 554 5.7.1 <relaytest@nmap.scanme.org>: Relay access denied		
33	192.168.20.141	192.168.20.140	SMTP	S: 554 5.7.1 <relaytest@nmap.scanme.org>: Relay access denied		
39	192.168.20.141	192.168.20.140	SMTP	S: 554 5.7.1 <relaytest@nmap.scanme.org>: Relay access denied		
45	192.168.20.141	192.168.20.140	SMTP	S: 554 5.7.1 <relaytest@nmap.scanme.org@[192.168.20.141]>: Rel		
51	192.168.20.141	192.168.20.140	SMTP	S: 554 5.7.1 <relaytest%nmap.scanme.org@metasploitable.locald		
57	192.168.20.141	192.168.20.140	SMTP	S: 554 5.7.1 <relaytest@nmap.scanme.org>: Relay access denied		
63	192.168.20.141	192.168.20.140	SMTP	S: 554 5.7.1 <relaytest%nmap.scanme.org>: Relay access denied		

SMTP open relay attack under progress

Display filters to identify SMTP relay attacks:

- `smtp.response.code == 554`: This indicates transaction has failed
- `smtp.response.code == 553`: This indicates invalid recipient
- `smtp matches "[a-zA-Z0-9._%+-]+@nmap.scanme.org"`: This displays filter to match the signature of Nmap while performing open relay test

 Another trick is to follow the TCP stream of the communication, as it might reflect some unusual sender or recipient addresses when an SMTP relay attack is under progress.

Important filters

The following filters can be used to detect any problem/errors in e-mail communications:

```
smtp.response.code >= 400
pop.response.indicator == "-ERR"
```

Display filters to look for e-mail credentials are as follows:

```
pop.request.command == "USER" || pop.request.command == "PASS"
imap.request contains "login"
smtp.req.command == "AUTH"
```

Summary

In this chapter, we solved SMTP forensics challenges using Wireshark and learned how to use Wireshark to detect attacks on e-mail communications, when conducted via popular security tools such as Metasploit and Nmap. In the next chapter, we will look at the malicious trace files and learn how to analyze them with the help of Wireshark.

5

Inspecting Malware Traffic

A malware is any software with malicious intents and generally refers to terms such as viruses, worms, Trojans, spywares, Adwares, Ransomwares, and so on. which we hear very often (unfortunately). Analyzing such a piece of software in order to understand the way it works, the files it affects, its unique signatures, and the harm it may cause to a system is called malware analysis. Malware analysis is a different ball game with its own set of tools than what we'll be digging into in this lesson. In this chapter, we will focus on the following:

- Analyze malicious traffic using Wireshark and some common sense
- Important pointers to nail down any malware on the network
- Understand how bots communicate over IRC
- Specifics to look for while analyzing spiteful IRC communication

The first question that might pop up in your head is "Why do I need to inspect malware traffic when my anti-virus and other solutions with the "blinking lights" completely protect me from such anomalies?". Well, if you think your security solutions protect you from anything and everything malicious, then I suggest you to come out of the fictitious world you've been living in and take a deep breath in reality. Also, reality says that no security solution can provide a 360-degree protection to your systems and network, as there will be times when these solutions can be circumvented and you need to take matters into your own hands and dig into the situation, with some assistance from the tools of course.

This is one of those situations. When you suspect that a system on your network is infected with a completely new and undetected malware and quite expectedly its signatures are not available or updated with the **antivirus (AV)** or **Intrusion Detection Systems (IDS)** solution in use. Otherwise, let's consider that your AV was smart enough to detect and delete it, but after a few days, the same problem echoes back. What do you do? Who do you go to? That is when you need to browse through the network traffic and analyze the malware yourself to nail the root cause.

One of the ways that IDS work is based on signatures. Analyzing malware traffic is analogous to the *behind the scenes* of a movie, as most of the signatures developed and integrated into an IDS to detect malicious traffic are based on the results derived from the network traffic analysis, and the humungous number of signatures developed on a regular basis is proof enough to comprehend its significance. In this chapter, we will emphasize on that precisely.

Gearing up Wireshark

To ease the analysis of malicious traffic, Wireshark requires certain tweaks. In short, we need to create a new profile in Wireshark to inspect malware traffic.

Updated columns

We added the following columns in Wireshark:

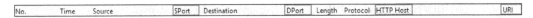

The columns can be added/modified by going to menu bar and navigating to **Edit | Preferences | Select Columns** (under **User Interface**).

- **SPort**—source port (unresolved)
- **DPort**—destination port (unresolved)
- **HTTP host**—display filter: `http.host`
- **URI**—display filter: `http.request.uri`

Updated coloring rules

For any packet containing an unusual number of DNS answers, we colored it with a background color — black and foreground color — orange, as can be seen in the following image.

No.	Time	Source	SPort	Destination	DPort	Length	Protocol
2346	17.03	172.16.165.2	53	172.16.165.132	57758	289	DNS

The coloring rule implied for any packet can be seen under the **Frame** header in the **Packet Details** pane.

```
[Coloring Rule Name: Unsual # of DNS Answers]
[Coloring Rule string: dns.count.answers > 5]
```

Coloring rule implied for the above packet

Important display filters

Some of the common display filters in use can be saved as well, as shown in the following filter toolbar:

| Filter: | | ⌄ Expression... | Clear | Apply | Save | HTTP Req | Host via DHCP | Host via DNS | IRC - Join Command | IRC - Requests |

Simply put the filter in the available space, wait until the background turns *green*, and click on **Save** (next to **Apply**, in the filter toolbar). The following are the used display filters:

- HTTP request: `http.request`
- Host via DHCP: `bootp.option.hostname`
- Host via DNS: `dns.qry.name`
- The join command of IRC: `irc && tcp matches "(?i) join"`
- The requests command of IRC: `irc.request`

> This profile is a sample profile that is limited to the analysis needs of this chapter. Please feel free to update the profile according to your requirements.

Malicious traffic analysis

A periodic analysis of network traffic can help detect the presence of any malware-infected hosts on our network. There is no *one size fits all* approach to analyzing malware traffic as there can be varying factors, such as channel of communication, different signature of the exploits and payloads used, and much more which will affect the approach we take. We will look at the following case study of one of the most popular threats of its time and analyze the traffic generated by it.

Case study – Blackhole exploit kit

An exploit is a piece of code that takes advantage of a vulnerability and an exploit kit is a simply a toolset containing the exploit code and payloads to automate the process of compromising a system, and taking care of the post exploitation job.

Blackhole, an exploit kit, was the most prevalent web threat in the year 2012 and was released on an underground hacking forum, according to Wikipedia.

 To understand the functionality of this exploit kit, please refer to https://nakedsecurity.sophos.com/exploring-the-blackhole-exploit-kit/.

We will now take up the capture file containing the infected traffic and analyze it. During the analysis process, we will point out significant clues that will lead us to the root cause of infection.

 The capture file used here can be downloaded from http://www.malware-traffic-analysis.net/2013/07/21/index.html. This website is an excellent source as it contains a comprehensive database of trace files containing malicious traffic and is regularly updated by Brad, a passionate security researcher.

Protocols in action

To see the protocols in action, we can look at the **Protocol** hierarchy under the **Statistics** menu, and in the trace file we're working with, we can see the use of HTTP and HTTP2 protocols along with the use of SSL to encrypt the data in transit.

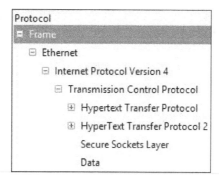

The IP address of the infected box

There are multiple ways that we can identify the infected machine's details. Checking for **TCP Conversations, Endpoints** and even for HTTP requests in this case can help us narrow down to the client (Infected Box).

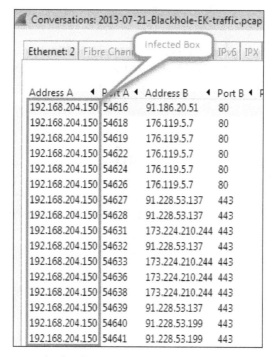

TCP conversations display that 192.168.204.150 was used in all the conversations

Since this trace contains HTTP traffic, filtering on the HTTP requests is a good choice to spot the client making the requests.

Filter:	http.request	
No.	Time	Source
4	0	192.168.204.150
13	0	192.168.204.150
24	1	192.168.204.150
99	3	192.168.204.150
112	3	192.168.204.150
119	8	192.168.204.150
175	9	192.168.204.150

Shows 192.168.204.150 is the source of all HTTP requests

In addition, if you have noticed that `192.168.204.150` is the only private IP address in the trace file, we can come to the following conclusion.

Infected machine's IP address: `192.168.204.150`

> If the trace file contained any DNS or DHCP traffic, even the host name of the victim can be found by filtering on NBNS/DNS traffic [dns.qry.name] or DHCP traffic [bootp.option.hostname].

Any unusual port number

If we look at the **TCP Conversations** and sort it based on the destination port in this case, that is, **Port B**, then we can clearly see that total three ports were used, that is, 80, 443, and 16471. Of these, 16471 looks odd because 80 and 443 are used for HTTP and HTTPS communication, and this completely justifies the protocols identified earlier.

A simple Google search out of curiosity reveals the following about port 16471.

> ### How to detect the ZeroAccess botnet on your network and ...
> scwoa.com/how-to-detect-the-zeroaccess-botnet-on-your-network-and-st... ▾
> Dec 11, 2013 - ZeroAccess (as of this writing) uses ports 16464, 16465, 16470, and / or
> 16471. The specific port depends on whether the version is 32-bit or ...
>
> ### [PDF] The ZeroAccess Botnet – Mining and Fraud for Massive ...
> cyber-peace.org/wp-content/uploads/.../Sophos_ZeroAccess_Botnet.pdf ▾
> by J Wyke - 2012 - Cited by 19 - Related articles
> Sep 4, 2012 - Ports 16464 and 16465 are used by the 32-bit and 64-bit versions of one
> botnet; ports 16470 and 16471 are used by the 64-bit and 32-bit ...

Unusual port number leads to information about ZeroAccess botnet

After researching further, we know that ZeroAccess Trojan is one of the payloads delivered by the Blackhole exploit kit.

Also, if we search for the IP address associated with port 16471, we will find the following result on `https://www.malwares.com/`:

Malicious URL History	Hostname Usage History	Malicious Sample Download History	Normal Sample Download History	Malicious Sample Communication History	Normal Sample Communication History
0	0	0	0	27	2

Malicious sample history communicated with this IP

No.	SHA-256	Anti-virus	Scan Date
27	2144D81A9EACBD6D90F72A547E4AE7547F6ED727711F6AE17F327E7665D546E1	35 / 47	2015-01-26 01:37:06
26	A8D136368FA08EE00266857CAB92FD7D2290B42611C1FA28DA47B5C926E45F81	46 / 53	2014-05-27 01:23:29
25	C3854C173EF08D75F5134691FEBC78A75B054E170CE387085A0D28D4208BE705	14 / 46	2013-08-17 03:45:19
24	BEF57360968571756223311BC86C5CFEB3955F0044C1706F0A492E49C61F5369	8 / 46	2013-08-14 15:52:43

Shows communication history of IP: 92.55.86.251

 Online resources are available to verify whether any domain/URL or IP address is blacklisted as well. A couple of good resources are:
`https://www.malwares.com/`
`https://www.virustotal.com/`

A compromised website

After analyzing the details above, for example, use of HTTP for communication, we may conclude that the client visited a malicious website, which began the whole catastrophe. For nailing the website or domain that the client visited, we will first need to check all the domains present in the trace file and connect the dots. Since there is no DNS traffic in this trace file, we can look at the domains by filtering on HTTP traffic. The following display filters are helpful in this case:

```
http.request
http.host
```

The following screenshot shows the host details:

```
Host
tonerkozpont.com
raiwinners.org
domenicossos.com
domenicossos.com
domenicossos.com
domenicossos.com
domenicossos.com
domenicossos.com
domenicossos.com
```

The list of domains under the Host column filtered by `http.host`

After analyzing the traffic from each domain, we can claim the following:

1. The client visited `http://tonerkozpont.hu/` and was redirected to `raiwinners.org`, as can be seen here:

```
<html>
<head>
<meta http-equiv="Refresh" content="1;URL="http://raiwinners.org/sword/in.cgi?2">
</head>
<body>
```

Redirected URL visible by the following TCP stream on packet 4

2. Also, if we follow that redirection request onto packet 13, we note another redirection to `domenicossos.com` via **Location** header in HTTP 302 response.

```
HTTP/1.1 302 Found
Date: Thu, 18 Jul 2013 20:45:33 GMT
Server: nginx/0.7.67
Location: http://domenicossos.com/ngen/controlling/mydb.php
Connection: Keep-Alive
```

Another redirection by the following TCP stream on packet 13

Another indication for the infected website can be seen in the **Flow Graph** under the **Statistics** menu. The graph indicates that the client visited `91.186.20.51` initially and this IP address resolved to `http://tonerkozpont.hu/`.

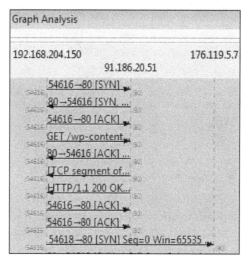

The Flow Graph indicating that 91.186.20.51 was visited first

Compromised website: `tonerkozpont.com` (`91.186.20.51`)

Infected file(s)

In this section, we will extract the files from the Wireshark capture, give the files an appropriate extension and test them for any inappropriate content.

Extracting files from a Wireshark capture can either be done manually or by going to **File | Export Objects | HTTP** to extract files from HTTP traffic as HTTP was used for communication in this case.

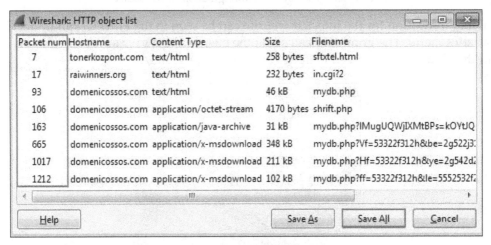

Packet num	Hostname	Content Type	Size	Filename
7	tonerkozpont.com	text/html	258 bytes	sftxtel.html
17	raiwinners.org	text/html	232 bytes	in.cgi?2
93	domenicossos.com	text/html	46 kB	mydb.php
106	domenicossos.com	application/octet-stream	4170 bytes	shrift.php
163	domenicossos.com	application/java-archive	31 kB	mydb.php?IMugUQWjIXMtBPs=kOYtJQ
665	domenicossos.com	application/x-msdownload	348 kB	mydb.php?Vf=53322f312h&be=2g522j3:
1017	domenicossos.com	application/x-msdownload	211 kB	mydb.php?Hf=53322f312h&ye=2g542d:
1212	domenicossos.com	application/x-msdownload	102 kB	mydb.php?ff=53322f312h&le=5552532f:

The HTTP object list for this trace file

> For a good link to understand how to extract file(s) manually, you can refer to `http://digital-forensics.sans.org/blog/2009/03/10/pulling-binaries-from-pcaps/`.

Steps to extract the file are as follows:

1. Click on **Save All** under the HTTP object list. This will save all the HTTP objects in the selected location. The next step will be to identify the type/extension of these files.

2. To identify the extension of the extracted files, we will need to first spot the packet number from the highlighted column in preceding screenshot and then navigate to the **Packets List** pane and right-click the packet to select **Follow TCP Stream**.

Next, we will assign appropriate file extensions to the extracted files. The following are the TCP streams of the files, highlighting the file extensions:

File 1 was a java-archive file extracted from the TCP stream of packet 163, as highlighted in the following screenshot:

```
HTTP/1.1 200 OK
Date: Thu, 18 Jul 2013 20:45:40 GMT
ETag: "f472177c3d4f8d76cacb20c3a092a2cc"
Server: nginx/0.7.67
Connection: Keep-Alive
Content-Type: application/java-archive
X-Powered-By: PHP/5.3.23
```

The files 2, 3, and 4 are the three executable files that were extracted from the TCP stream of packet 665 They are mentioned as follows:

```
HTTP/1.1 200 OK
Date: Thu, 18 Jul 2013 20:45:42 GMT
Pragma: public
Server: nginx/0.7.67
Expires: Thu, 18 Jul 2013 23:42:19 GMT
Connection: Keep-Alive
Content-Type: application/x-msdownload
X-Powered-By: PHP/5.3.23
Cache-Control: must-revalidate, post-check=0, pre-check=0
Cache-Control: private
Content-Length: 348160
Content-Disposition: attachment; filename="calc.exe"
Content-Transfer-Encoding: binary                    File-signature for EXE

MZ...................@.................................!..L.!This
program cannot be run in DOS mode.
```

First executable file, named calc.exe

The second file is as follows:

```
Content-Length: 211968
Content-Disposition: attachment; filename="info.exe"
Content-Transfer-Encoding: binary                    File-signature for EXE

MZ...................@.................................!..L.!This
program cannot be run in DOS mode.
```

Second executable file, named info.exe

The third file is as follows:

```
Content-Length: 102912
Content-Disposition: attachment; filename="readme.exe"
Content-Transfer-Encoding: binary                    File-signature for EXE

MZ...................@.................................!..L.!This
program cannot be run in DOS mode.
```

Third executable file, named readme.exe

After successfully extracting and giving appropriate name and extension to files, we have the following:

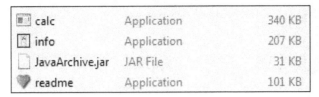

calc	Application	340 KB
info	Application	207 KB
JavaArchive.jar	JAR File	31 KB
readme	Application	101 KB

Significant files extracted from the trace file

Now, the process of analyzing the files is up to you. Our options in this case are:

- The file can either be sent to specialists who can reverse-engineer it and narrow down any anomalies, such as a call for payload
- The files can be uploaded to a website that checks for suspicious signatures.

The following is a sample report after uploading readme.exe on https://www.virustotal.com/.

SHA256:	43565420246215bef3f02615166e38eaec4cde9d77c59f322c99421d1693649c
File name:	readme.exe
Detection ratio:	36 / 49

36 of the 49 AV vendors detected this file as malicious

Conclusion

In this case study, we came to the following conclusion:

The client/victim (192.168.204.150) visited an infected website (http://tonerkozpont.hu/) that had redirected him further to a website (domenicossos.com) hosting the Blackhole exploit kit on mydb.php page. The suspicious website then downloaded the java exploit (JavaArchive.jar) on the victim box and then delivered three different payloads (calc.exe, info.exe, and readme.exe). Once infected, additional HTTPS traffic was noted for multiple subdomains of ohtheigh.cc and also traffic to port 16471 was present, which pointed to ZeroAccess Trojan.

IRC botnet(s)

Internet Relay Chat (IRC), is a chat system used to communicate over the Internet, while a botnet is a network of compromised machines (bots), which is remotely controlled by an attacker using a **command and control (C&C)** server. IRC is the most popular C&C channel used by botnets.

[The presence of IRC on a corporate network should raise a *red alert!*]

Simply put, once a machine is compromised, it is programmed to connect to a preset IRC channel and wait for further instructions from the server. An attacker can then remotely control the compromised bot to perform actions on his or her behalf, and in the worst case scenario, an attacker can use multiple bots together and perform a catastrophic attack such as a **Distributed Denial of Service (DDoS)**(an attack against the *availability* of information under the umbrella of the popular CIA triad) against the target of choice.

[Refer to the following, for a better understanding of:

IRC communications: `https://tools.ietf.org/html/rfc1459`

botnet-based communications: `http://honeynet.org/papers/bots/`]

Inspection

For the purpose of analysis, we will pick up a trace file from `https://mcfp.felk.cvut.cz/publicDatasets/CTU-Malware-Capture-Botnet-45/botnet-capture-20110815-rbot-dos-icmp.pcap`.

1. Since, we expect this to be IRC communication, then using an appropriate display filter can prove handy, and the output is shown here:

| Filter: | irc | | | | | | ☑ Expression... | Clear | Apply |

No.	Time	Source	SPort	Destination	DPort	Length	Protocol
46	19.02	147.32.84.165	1039	130.239.18.172	6667	101	IRC
47	19.06	130.239.18.172	6667	147.32.84.165	1039	118	IRC
58	19.22	130.239.18.172	6667	147.32.84.165	1039	159	IRC

By default, frames communicating over port 6667 are decoded as IRC in Wireshark

> Sometimes, attackers might use an unusual port for IRC communication. An indicator in that case will be the visibility of popular IRC commands as USER, NICK, JOIN, MODE, and USERHOST. Then, we will need to manually set Wireshark to decode such traffic as IRC by selecting **Decode As** under **Analyze** in the menu bar and select the appropriate setting for decoding.

2. Filtering on DNS communications show us the packets based on the coloring rule (dns.count.answers>5) defined earlier. It can be seen as follows:

| 42 | 18.98 | 147.32.80.9 | | 53 147.32.84.165 | 1025 | 479 DNS | Standard query response 0x3e54 CNAME chat.freenode.net |
| 28627 | 795.26 | 147.32.80.9 | | 53 147.32.84.165 | 1025 | 479 DNS | Standard query response 0x3453 CNAME chat.freenode.net |

DNS responses received in the colored packets highlight that they contained more than five answers in the DNS response. The DNS answers from the trace file are as follows:

```
⊟ Answers
  ⊞ irc.freenode.net: type CNAME, class IN, cname chat.freenode.net
  ⊞ chat.freenode.net: type A, class IN, addr 130.239.18.172
  ⊞ chat.freenode.net: type A, class IN, addr 140.211.167.98
  ⊞ chat.freenode.net: type A, class IN, addr 140.211.167.99
  ⊞ chat.freenode.net: type A, class IN, addr 174.143.119.91
  ⊞ chat.freenode.net: type A, class IN, addr 213.92.8.4
  ⊞ chat.freenode.net: type A, class IN, addr 213.179.58.83
  ⊞ chat.freenode.net: type A, class IN, addr 213.232.93.3
  ⊞ chat.freenode.net: type A, class IN, addr 216.155.130.130
  ⊞ chat.freenode.net: type A, class IN, addr 38.229.70.20
  ⊞ chat.freenode.net: type A, class IN, addr 78.40.125.4
  ⊞ chat.freenode.net: type A, class IN, addr 82.96.64.4
  ⊞ chat.freenode.net: type A, class IN, addr 86.65.39.15
  ⊞ chat.freenode.net: type A, class IN, addr 89.16.176.16
  ⊞ chat.freenode.net: type A, class IN, addr 93.152.160.101
  ⊞ chat.freenode.net: type A, class IN, addr 128.237.157.136
```

3. As IRC traffic traverses in plaintext; therefore, performing a **Follow TCP Stream** on IRC traffic is a good bet to track the activities and IRC commands executed by the bot.

```
NICK Pepe889696
USER znuehjm 0 0 :Pepe889696
USERHOST Pepe889696
MODE Pepe889696 -x
JOIN #zarasa48
```

- ° NICK: This is used to give user a nickname or change an already existing nickname
- ° USER: This is used at the beginning of connection to specify the username, hostname, server name, and real name of a new user
- ° USERHOST: This is a command that takes nickname as a parameter and returns information about it
- ° MODE: This command is used to change the mode of a username or a channel
- ° JOIN: This command is used to join or connect to a specific IRC channel

Digging up further into the TCP stream led us to the following:

```
:pepe|2!~kvirc@cmpgw-27.felk.cvut.cz PRIVMSG #zarasa48 :.ddos.syn 147.32.96.69 1
:pepe|2!~kvirc@cmpgw-27.felk.cvut.cz PRIVMSG #zarasa48 :.ddos.syn 147.32.96.69 1 60
PRIVMSG #zarasa48 :[DDoS]: Done with flood (0KB/sec).
PRIVMSG #zarasa48 :[DDoS]: Flooding: (147.32.96.69:1) for 60 seconds.
:pepe|2!~kvirc@cmpgw-27.felk.cvut.cz PRIVMSG #zarasa48 :.tcpflood syn 147.32.96.69 1
1000
PRIVMSG #zarasa48 :[TCP]: Error sending packets to IP: 147.32.96.69. Packets sent:
0. Returned: <0>.
PRIVMSG #zarasa48 :[TCP]: Normal syn flooding: (147.32.96.69:1) for 1000 seconds.
:pepe|2!~kvirc@cmpgw-27.felk.cvut.cz PRIVMSG #zarasa48 :.tcpflood syn 147.32.96.69 1
100
PRIVMSG #zarasa48 :[TCP]: Error sending packets to IP: 147.32.96.69. Packets sent:
0. Returned: <0>.
PRIVMSG #zarasa48 :[TCP]: Normal syn flooding: (147.32.96.69:1) for 100 seconds.
:pepe|2!~kvirc@cmpgw-27.felk.cvut.cz PRIVMSG #zarasa48 :.tcpflood syn 147.32.96.69
22 100
PRIVMSG #zarasa48 :[TCP]: Error sending packets to IP: 147.32.96.69. Packets sent:
0. Returned: <0>.
PRIVMSG #zarasa48 :[TCP]: Normal syn flooding: (147.32.96.69:22) for 100 seconds.
:pepe|2!~kvirc@cmpgw-27.felk.cvut.cz PRIVMSG #zarasa48 :.dos.random 147.32.96.69 22
1000
:pepe|2!~kvirc@cmpgw-27.felk.cvut.cz PRIVMSG #zarasa48 :.ddos.random 147.32.96.69 22
1000
PRIVMSG #zarasa48 :[DDoS]: Done with flood (0KB/sec).
PRIVMSG #zarasa48 :[DDoS]: Flooding: (147.32.96.69:22) for 1000 seconds.
:pepe|2!~kvirc@cmpgw-27.felk.cvut.cz PRIVMSG #zarasa48 :.tcpflood ack 147.32.96.69
337 120 -r
PRIVMSG #zarasa48 :[TCP]: Error sending packets to IP: 147.32.96.69. Packets sent:
0. Returned: <0>.
PRIVMSG #zarasa48 :[TCP]: Spoofed ack flooding: (147.32.96.69:337) for 120 seconds.
:pepe|2!~kvirc@cmpgw-27.felk.cvut.cz PRIVMSG #zarasa48 :.icmpflood 147.32.96.69 1800
PRIVMSG #zarasa48 :[ICMP]: Flooding: (147.32.96.69) for 1800 seconds.
```

Several PRIVMSG commands were issued by the C&C server to perform a DoS attack.

Summary

In this chapter, we learned how to use Wireshark to look for and put together the different pieces of the malware traffic analysis puzzle and also elaborated on IRC botnet-infected communication. In the next chapter, we will look at how to use Wireshark to meet our network performance needs.

6
Network Performance Analysis

Network uptime and optimum performance are a prime concern for any technician, and the issues that affect it could be one of many numerous issues, and completely depends on the size and complexity of the network under question. These anomalies can include the following, but are not restricted to them:

- Slow Internet
- Bottlenecks
- Loss of packets and/or retransmissions
- Excessive bandwidth consumption
- Unexpected BitTorrent traffic

An in-depth understanding of how the network protocols intertwine and work is indispensable to troubleshooting the network for performance issues. For example, if we don't understand TCP's flow and error control mechanism effectively, then we may not be able to efficiently test for TCP-based performance issues.

Many a time, I have had people ask me, "How can Wireshark fix my network issues?" Well, an honest answer to that would be that Wireshark might not always lead you to the root cause of the problem, but it can definitely help you detect its location. Narrowing down the cause of the problem is totally up to the skills of the analyst. As an example, Wireshark may help you locate the device that is dropping packets on the network but might not always lead you to the reason behind it.

Some of the features of Wireshark that assist in analyzing for performance issues are as follows:

- Expert Infos window
- Graphs
- Time variations
- Colorization rules

Creating a custom profile for troubleshooting

We will first go ahead and create a rock-solid profile for the purpose of troubleshooting and then take a look at the different issues that might hinder network performance.

By now, I assume that you're comfortable with creating profiles in Wireshark. The highlights of the profile are as follows:

1. Uncheck/disable the **Allow subdissector to reassemble TCP streams** option. This should only be enabled while getting the HTTP or SMB objects.

2. To deal with sequencing issues in TCP, we first need to enable **Analyze TCP sequence numbers** under **Preferences | Protocols | TCP**. The following is how my TCP Preferences look like:

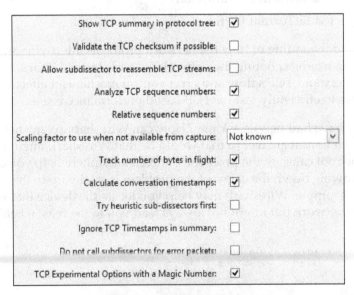

Troubleshooting profile: TCP Preferences

Next, put the sequence number, next sequence number, and acknowledgment number into three different columns in Wireshark for ease of analyzing the TCP sequencing as shown in the next screenshot.

3. "Time" is always a major factor when looking for delays on the network and hence we will begin by tweaking it. First of all, we will change the display format of time by navigating to **View | Time Display Format** and selecting **Seconds since previously displayed packet**.

   Now, include the delta time column (`tcp.time_delta`) next to the already present **Time** column, as shown in the next screenshot.

4. Include another column for the window size (`tcp.window_size`) to check for any issues related to the TCP windowing process, as shown in the next screenshot.

5. Create and save the following display filter buttons:

   ° **HTTP Errors**: `http.response.code > 399`

   ° **DNS Errors**: `dns.flags.rcode > 0`

   ° **FTP Errors**: `ftp.response.code > 399`

   ° **WLAN Retries**: `wlan.fc.retry == 1`

Troubleshooting profile: columns and saved display filters

The preceding profile is a sample troubleshooting profile. Hence, please feel free to add and/or modify this as per your environment. As an example, you may want to update this based on signatures from Torrent-based traffic.

Optimization before analysis

Choosing the right place to begin capturing is most often the key to resolving performance setbacks. For example, it is advisable to place the analyzer closer to the system of the employee who is regularly complaining about poor network performance than placing it at any random user's system, as this will give us a better insight to the problem.

If capturing at the server is our only option, then we need to make sure that we use a good set of capture filters to avoid any unwanted traffic, or we may choose to extract the relevant conversation(s) from the complete trace file with the use of display filters.

For example, if we are only interested in traffic to or from a particular host with IP address 10.1.0.20, then we can use host 10.1.0.20 as our capture filter, or after capturing the complete traffic, we can use ip.host == 10.1.0.20 as a display filter and use **Export Specified Packets** to extract that conversation.

This is important and saves a lot of analysis time by avoiding irrelevant frames.

Another recommendation is to use command-line tools, such as tshark or tcpdump, if the capture needs to be performed for a longer duration.

TCP-based issues

The **Expert Infos** tab is a pretty good indicator of any problems that occur due to issues with TCP; otherwise, we can also use the display filter, tcp.analysis.flags, to narrow down any TCP issues identified by Wireshark. The following are some commonly faced TCP problems and their respective display filters:

- Previous segment not captured (tcp.analysis.lost_segment)
- Duplicate ACKs (tcp.analysis.duplicate_ack)
- TCP fast retransmissions (tcp.analysis.fast_retransmission)
- TCP retransmissions (tcp.analysis.retransmission)
- Out-of-order Segments (tcp.analysis.out_of_order)
- Zero window (tcp.analysis.zero_window)

The important points to note are:

- Whenever packets are being lost on the network, we will note fast retransmissions and/or retransmissions on the wire. The general rule of thumb is that duplicate ACKs lead to fast retransmissions and expired **Request Time-Outs (RTOs)** at the sender leads to retransmissions.

Expert Infos window indicating fast retransmissions and retransmissions under the Notes tab

- When an application runs over TCP, we can detect path and server latency by looking at the delay between the SYN and SYN/ACK (path latency) and delay between an ACK from the server and the actual data that follows, for example, delay in DNS responses for server latencies, if any.

- Whenever Wireshark detects any side of the TCP conversation advertising a TCP window size value (`tcp.window_size_value == 0`) as 0, it marks the packet as **Zero window**. This condition is caused when the recipient's receive buffer cannot keep up with the rate of data reception. The point to note here is that if the packets have RST, SYN, or FIN bits set to 1, they will not be marked as **Zero window**, as shown here:

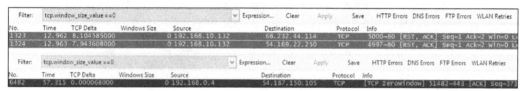

Zero window example

Case study 1 – Slow Internet

One of the employees at our organization approached the network support geek (let's call him Bob) with a request to check whether there were any issues with the Internet, as he had been receiving very slow response from applications over the Internet over the past couple of days. After some investigation from his end, Bob found out that this was a widespread issue and many people had noted this in the past two days.

Since the issue was with the Internet (as per the analysis and viewpoint of users), Bob decided to first connect the analyzer to the exit node, that is, the router, connecting the network to the Internet and to capture some traffic for analysis.

Analysis

Most of the traffic in the trace file was coming to and from a particular host 192.168.10.132, hence Bob filtered on ip.host==192.168.10.132 and exported those packets into a different trace file for analysis.

The **Conversations** window indicated a large number of TCP and UDP conversations in a short span of time in which the frames were captured. After sorting on the **Bytes** column under the UDP tab; Bob noted communication occurring over the same port on the client, that is, **46816** to different IP addresses.

UDP Conversations							
Address A ◀	Port A ◀	Address B ◀	Port B ◀	Packets ◀	Bytes ▼	Packets A→B ◀	Bytes A→B ◀
192.168.10.132	46816	182.58.215.46	17940	471	372 354	300	360 583
192.168.10.132	46816	116.203.219.84	31098	283	231 847	168	224 215
192.168.10.132	46816	2.51.48.167	26372	109	41 966	57	3 534

Further, looking at the DNS queries, it was found that queries were being made to domains of different countries and was hinted toward the use of Vuze (a BitTorrent client) as a potential culprit:

```
DNS     Standard query 0xb445   A version.vuze.com
DNS     Standard query 0x10c7   SOA piyush-40f60e5d.docomo.com
DNS     Standard query 0x0001   ANY tracker.istole.it
DNS     Standard query 0x0001   ANY 12.rarbg.me
DNS     Standard query 0x0002   ANY tracker.istole.it
DNS     Standard query 0xdc47   A ipv4.tracker.harry.lu
DNS     Standard query 0x2746   A tracker.coppersurfer.tk
DNS     Standard query 0x5e40   A bttracker.crunchbanglinux.org
DNS     Standard query 0x2943   A tracker1.wasabii.com.tw
DNS     Standard query 0xae4d   A tracker.nwps.ws
DNS     Standard query 0x6b4c   A tracker.ccc.de
```

DNS queries

Both these indicators were strong enough for Bob to physically go over to that system (192.168.10.132) and check. He found that the user was running the BitTorrent client and downloading stuff via Torrents. Once the download was stopped and Vuze was uninstalled from the user's machine, everything worked fine, and the users received optimum Internet speed.

Case study 2 – Sluggish downloads

In this case study, we will look at a trace file that contains frames from a download occurring at the system of a user who was complaining about sluggish downloads.

Analysis

After simulating the same download that the user performed and capturing traffic at his system, we came up with a huge trace file and hence filtered the traffic (using **tshark**) on a particular IP from which the download was streamed.

The first thing to note when checking for latencies is the delta time and, more specifically, the TCP delta time when downloading over TCP. Sorting the traffic on TCP delta time, we see a significant delay in time, as highlighted here:

No.	Time	TCP Delta ▼
278630	191.901	19.821587000
278309	191.754	19.689591000
278143	191.678	19.581039000
278151	191.682	19.575095000
278115	191.666	19.554924000
277988	191.625	19.534762000
277805	191.525	19.382842000
277185	191.244	19.136907000
276868	191.103	19.002715000
257247	166.221	18.860083000

High TCP delta time

A graph can also be created indicating the high TCP delta time, which can be imperative for showing and explaining the problems to others.

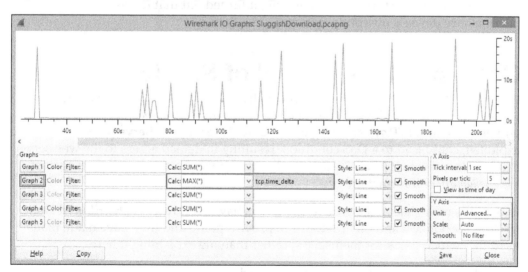

This graph can be generated by performing the following steps:

1. Go to **Statistics | IO Graph**.
2. Under the **Y Axis** section, select **Advanced** from the **Unit** drop-down menu.
3. Select **MAX(*)** from the **Calc** drop-down menu and enter the required filter (`tcp.time_delta`) for TCP delta time.
4. Click on the **Graph 2** button on the extreme left.

Next, we can look at the **Expert Infos** window, to see if Wireshark detected any errors in the trace file. The following were the observations:

- **Previous segment not captured**: 1309 frames
- **Duplicate ACKs**: 12249 frames
- **TCP fast retransmissions**: 625 frames
- **TCP retransmissions**: 1216 frames
- **Out-of-order segments**: 1226 frames
- **Zero window**: 3 frames

To identify the location of the packet loss, we decided to analyze the TCP sequencing numbers (the three columns, **SEQ#**, **NEXTSEQ#**, and **ACK#** that we added to the profile earlier) and concluded that packet loss occurred close to the client, and after further investigation, it turned out that it was due to an intermediary device's misconfiguration.

Case study 3 – Denial of Service

Denial of Service (DoS) is an attack in which access to the service(s) is denied to authorized personnel when they need it. For example, the recently discovered vulnerability in HTTP.sys affecting the **Internet Information Server (IIS)**, if exploited, could lead to a DoS condition, resulting in denied access to the web server that is vulnerable to it (CVE-2015-1635). In simpler words, this is an attack against the *availability* of information.

In the past, many hacktivist groups or hackers have performed a **Distributed DoS (DDoS)** for political and other reasons to prove a point, and they have made many headlines which speak for themselves, rather than me explaining it here.

Let's take a look at a pretty standard DoS attack and analyze it via Wireshark.

SYN flood

An SYN flood attack is an attack when an attacker sends a huge number of TCP frames with SYN bit set to 1, indicating that he/she is trying to initiate a connection. However, when a server receives such requests in a large number and in a very short duration, this tends to drain out its resources; hence, legitimate users are unable to use that particular service, resulting in a DoS condition.

The following is a trace indicating an SYN flood attack on a web server using the `hping3` utility.

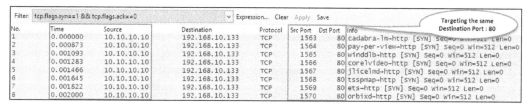

An SYN flood attack under process

 A useful display filter to check for SYN flood attacks is:
```
tcp.flags.syn==1 && tcp.flags.ack==0
```

Summary

In this chapter, we looked at how to create a relevant troubleshooting profile and learned how to use the TCP delta time to sort on any time latencies, as well as the IO Graph for better representation of the performance problems. The key to troubleshooting still remains an in-depth understanding of protocols because a tool can only help us sort things out, but it is our job to figure out what to look for.

Index

Telnet 39
Telnet traffic
  credentials, viewing for 39
TFTP 41
tools, of trade
  defining 4
  Nagios Network Analyzer 4
  OmniPeek 4
  Tcpdump 4
  Wireshark 4
tools, Wireshark
  about 59
  Pcap2XML 62, 63
  SSHFlow 63
  Sysdig 61
  Xplico 59, 60
traffic
  analyzing 94
tshark
  about 33, 109
  capture, saving to file 34
  capture, starting 33
  filters, using 34
  statistics 34

W

WEP
  cracking 70
Wireshark
  about 4
  command-line utilities 32
  defining 5, 88
  display filters 89

essential techniques 27
features 104
filtering through 19, 20
updated coloring rules 89
updated columns 88
URL 4, 5
used, for defining first packet
      capture 15-17
using 68
Wireshark interface
  about 6
  Capture frame 9-12
  Capture Help menu 13
  Files menu 13, 14
  filter toolbar 7, 8
  main toolbar 7
  Menu bar 6
  online resources 14
  Status bar 14
  title 6
Wireshark profiles
  about 25
  creating 25, 26

X

Xplico
  about 59, 60
  installing 59

Z

ZeroAccess Trojan 98
Zero window 107

Thank you for buying
Wireshark Network Security

About Packt Publishing

Packt, pronounced 'packed', published its first book, *Mastering phpMyAdmin for Effective MySQL Management*, in April 2004, and subsequently continued to specialize in publishing highly focused books on specific technologies and solutions.

Our books and publications share the experiences of your fellow IT professionals in adapting and customizing today's systems, applications, and frameworks. Our solution-based books give you the knowledge and power to customize the software and technologies you're using to get the job done. Packt books are more specific and less general than the IT books you have seen in the past. Our unique business model allows us to bring you more focused information, giving you more of what you need to know, and less of what you don't.

Packt is a modern yet unique publishing company that focuses on producing quality, cutting-edge books for communities of developers, administrators, and newbies alike. For more information, please visit our website at www.packtpub.com.

About Packt Open Source

In 2010, Packt launched two new brands, Packt Open Source and Packt Enterprise, in order to continue its focus on specialization. This book is part of the Packt Open Source brand, home to books published on software built around open source licenses, and offering information to anybody from advanced developers to budding web designers. The Open Source brand also runs Packt's Open Source Royalty Scheme, by which Packt gives a royalty to each open source project about whose software a book is sold.

Writing for Packt

We welcome all inquiries from people who are interested in authoring. Book proposals should be sent to author@packtpub.com. If your book idea is still at an early stage and you would like to discuss it first before writing a formal book proposal, then please contact us; one of our commissioning editors will get in touch with you.

We're not just looking for published authors; if you have strong technical skills but no writing experience, our experienced editors can help you develop a writing career, or simply get some additional reward for your expertise.

Network Analysis using Wireshark Cookbook

ISBN: 978-1-84951-764-5   Paperback: 452 pages

Over 80 recipes to analyze and troubleshoot network problems using Wireshark

1. Place Wireshark in the network and configure it for effective network analysis.

2. Use Wireshark's powerful statistical tools and expert system for pinpointing network problems.

3. Use Wireshark for troubleshooting network performance, applications, and security problems in the network.

Wireshark Essentials

ISBN: 978-1-78355-463-8   Paperback: 194 pages

Get up and running with Wireshark to analyze network packets and protocols effectively

1. Troubleshoot problems, identify security risks, and measure key application performance metrics with Wireshark.

2. Gain valuable insights into the network and application protocols, and the key fields in each protocol.

3. Configure Wireshark, and analyze networks and applications at the packet level with the help of practical examples and step-wise instructions.

open source
community experience distilled

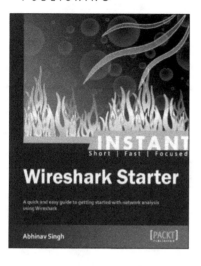

Instant Wireshark Starter

ISBN: 978-1-84969-564-0   Paperback: 68 pages

A quick and easy guide to getting started with
network analysis using Wireshark

1. Learn something new in an Instant!
   A short, fast, focused guide delivering
   immediate results.

2. Documents key features and tasks that
   can be performed using Wireshark.

3. Covers details of filters, statistical analysis,
   and other important tasks.

Lync Server Cookbook

ISBN: 978-1-78217-347-2   Paperback: 392 pages

Over 90 recipes to empower you to configure,
integrate, and manage your very own Lync
Server deployment

1. Customize and manage Lync security and
   authentication on cloud and mobile.

2. Discover the best ways to integrate Lync
   with Exchange and explore resource forests.

3. The book is designed to teach you how to
   select the best tools, debugging methods, and
   monitoring options to help you in your
   day-to-day work.

Please check **www.PacktPub.com** for information on our titles

www.ingramcontent.com/pod-product-compliance
Lightning Source LLC
Chambersburg PA
CBHW060150060326
40690CB00018B/4056